Grade 2

Wonders

CALIFORNIA Content Reader

B

The **McGraw·Hill** Companies

 Macmillan/McGraw-Hill

Published by Macmillan/McGraw-Hill, of McGraw-Hill Education, a division of The McGraw-Hill Companies, Inc.,
Two Penn Plaza, New York, New York 10121.

Printed in the United States of America

11 12 13 14 15 16 17 18 WEB 20 19 18 17 16 15 14 13

Contents

Contents

4

How Can You Describe Where Something Is?

Position is the place where something is. You can tell the position of an object by comparing it to something that does not move. You can use words such as above, below, left, right, near, far, next, to, in, on, and under to describe position. What other words describe position?

▼ The orange fish is to the left of the chest.

When something moves, its position changes. You can describe its new position by comparing it to other objects or to what is in the background.

▼ Where is the orange fish now? How did it move?

Poetry in Motion

Doing a backflip on a bicycle is all in a day's work for one amazing rider.

How do you get from one place to another on a bicycle? Most people travel on the ground. But some riders fly through the air!

How many different bicycles do you see in this picture? The right answer is just one. This is really many pictures taken in just a few seconds. All of them show the same bicycle in motion. The rider is doing a backflip in the air!

He starts his ride on the right side of the picture. He takes off from a brown ramp. He lands on the pile of sand on the left side of the picture.

Seb Rogers/Alamy

The rider starts a backflip by leaning back. Find the first place in the picture where he leans back. Here is a hint: His front wheel is pointing at the sky. His back wheel is pointing at the ground.

In the middle of the backflip, the rider is upside down. Find the place in this picture where he is upside down. How can you tell? Look at his helmet. When the rider is upside down, his helmet is pointing at the ground! Both of his bicycle's wheels are pointing at the sky.

Now find the spot that shows the rider landing. How can you tell? To tell the position of an object, look around it. When the rider lands, his wheels touch the ground. The front wheel lands first. The rider is no longer high above the truck and the ramp .

It takes a lot of practice to learn this trick. This rider is an expert! — *Susan Moger*

Compare/Contrast Writing Frame

Use the Writing Frame below to orally summarize "How Can You Describe Where Something Is?"

The photographs on these pages are **like** each other in many ways. They are the **same** because _____

_____ .

The photographs are also **similar** because they **both** _____

_____ .

In one way, though, the photographs are **different**.

They are **different** because _____

_____ .

So the photographs on these pages are the **same** in many ways, but also **different** in one way.

. . . .

Use the frame to write the summary on another sheet of paper. Be sure to include the **bold** signal words. Keep this as a model of this Text Structure.

Critical Thinking

1 The place where something is can be called its

_____ .

    A. position

    B. grade

    C. planet

2 Find the words that describe position in "How Can You Describe Where Something Is?"

3 Point out the text on page 7 that tells how to describe a new position of something.

4 Find the first photograph in "How Can You Describe Where Something Is?" and read aloud the caption.

> A caption is a title or an explanation of a photograph.

Digital Learning

For a list of links and activities that relate to this Science standard, visit the California Treasures Web site at www.macmillanmh.com to access the Content Reader resources.

Have children view the e-Review "How Can You Describe Where Something Is?"

EL In addition, distribute copies of the Translated Concept Summaries in Spanish, Chinese, Hmong, Khmer, and Vietnamese.

Objects in Motion

When something is moving, it is in **motion**. Motion is a change in position. The diver shown is in motion. Her position changes as she moves from the top of the diving board to the pool.

What Are Forces?

You have to use force to put something in motion. A push or a pull is a force that can put something in motion. If you push something, it will move away from you. A kick is a kind of push. To pull something moves it closer to you. When you open a drawer, you pull. How much strength or force is used to push or pull a thing determines how it moves.

A **simple machine** can help with the force of pushing or pulling something. A wheel is a simple machine. Because it rolls, it makes pushing and pulling things easier. A ramp is another simple machine. It is easier to push something up a ramp than it is to lift it.

▲ In this game, the children pull on each side of the rope.

Amazing Machines

Here is a look at some machines that will make you say "Wow!"

These new inventions are cool. They're fun. The inventors used their imaginations. They said, "What if we tried this?" Maybe you'll say, "What will they dream up next?"

Murata Boy

Murata Boy is the world's first bike-riding robot. Murata Boy has sensors in his body. He has a camera in his head. They keep him from falling down as he rides.

We use our feet to make a bike move. First we push on one pedal to make it go down. The other pedal comes up. We push on that pedal to make it go down. The pedals are connected to the bike's wheels. Pushing on the pedals turns the wheels. The harder we push, the faster we go.

Koichi Kamoshida/Getty Images

Diving Dolphin

Take a look at this machine. Where do you think you could use it? In the water, of course. How do you know? It looks like a dolphin. Dolphins use their fins and tails to move through the water. This machine does the same thing. The fins and tail make it move. The tail pushes back and forth against the water. The fins push up or down against the water.

Courtesy Structured Solutions II LLC

The Wovel

Have you ever shoveled snow? It is hard work! This machine makes it easier. It works like a seesaw. On a seesaw you and a friend go up and down. By pushing down on your side, you lift up your friend. When your friend comes down, you go up.

The Wovel is like a seesaw on a wheel. As you wheel it along, you push down on the handle. Pushing down raises the shovel. The shovel lifts up snow. Push down hard enough and the snow flies through the air. —*Susan Moger*

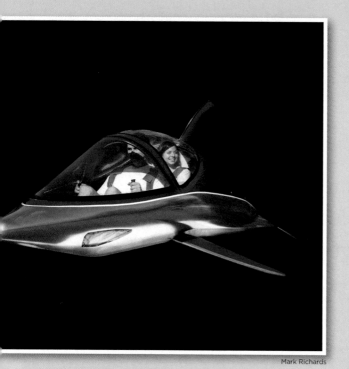

Mark Richards

TIME FOR KIDS

Cause/Effect Writing Frame

Use the Writing Frame below to orally summarize "Objects in Motion" and "What Are Forces?"

Motion is a change in position. Using force, you can put something in _____.

The **effect** of this is _____

_____.

If you push something that can move, **then** it will

_____.

If you pull something that can move, **then** it will

_____.

Therefore, when something moves, it does so because _____.

Use the frame to write the summary on another sheet of paper. Be sure to include the **bold** signal words. Keep this as a model of this Text Structure.

Critical Thinking

1 When something is moving, it is in _____.

   A. middle

   B. secret

   C. motion

2 Find the sentence in "What Are Forces?" that tells what happens when you push something.

3 Point out where on page 13 the text explains what determines how something moves.

4 Which photograph has a caption? Talk about this caption with a partner. What added information does it give that is not in the text?

A caption is a title or an explanation of a photograph.

Digital Learning

For a list of links and activities that relate to this Science standard, visit the California Treasures Web site at www.macmillanmh.com to access the Content Reader resources.

Have children view the Science in Motion video "How a Ball Changes Direction."

EL In addition, distribute copies of the Translated Concept Summaries in Spanish, Chinese, Hmong, Khmer, and Vietnamese.

Gravity

Gravity is a force that pulls things toward each other. All things have a force of gravity. The larger an object is, the stronger the force of gravity it has. Even though you can not see gravity, you can feel it. Gravity is what keeps you on the ground. It pulls you back to the ground when you jump into the air. Without gravity, you would fly into outer space.

   Earth has a strong force of gravity because of
its size. The gravity of Earth is stronger than the
gravity of smaller things. That is why a ball in
the air will fall back down to Earth.

Up in the Air

A brother and sister thrill thousands of people with their record-setting juggling act.

David Strick

Jugglers keep balls flying through the air. They throw the balls up. They catch them. Then they throw them up again. They never hold a ball for very long. The balls are always moving. The balls make patterns in the air. Why is this hard to do? The answer is gravity.

When you throw a ball up, gravity pulls it down. Gravity is a force. It pulls objects toward each other. Gravity pulls you down a slide. Gravity keeps your feet on the ground.

Vova and Olga Galchenko are jugglers. The brother and sister came to the United States from Russia. Vova was 15 and Olga was 12. They juggle on street corners. They juggle in contests. They juggle on TV shows. They were great jugglers when they came here. Now they may be the best jugglers ever. When they juggle, the Galchenkos seem to turn off gravity.

Vova and Olga started juggling when they were very young. They practiced and practiced. They juggled balls and clubs. Clubs look like thin rockets. They have long handles. Vova and Olga pass the clubs back and forth.

They can juggle up to 12 clubs at the same time. Practicing paid off. Now they hold world records for juggling clubs.

Vova and Olga say, "We are the only jugglers gravity fears." —*Susan Moger*

Vova and Olga keep 10 clubs in the air at one time.

David Strick

21

Description Writing Frame

Use the Writing Frame below to orally summarize "Gravity."

All things have a force of gravity. Gravity is _____

_____.

You can feel gravity. **For instance**, when you jump in the air, you can feel the force of gravity _____

_____.

Without gravity, you would _____

_____.

Earth has a strong force of gravity because of its size. **For example**, a ball in the air _____

_____.

Use the frame to write the summary on another sheet of paper. Be sure to include the **bold** signal words. Keep this as a model for this Text Structure.

Critical Thinking

1 A force that pulls things toward each other is

called _____.

    A. space

    B. gravy

    C. gravity

2 Point to the sentences in "Up in the Air" that tell what Vova and Olga Galchenko do.

3 Find the sentence in this article that tells how many clubs Vova and Olga can juggle at the same time.

A diagram is a drawing or a plan. It explains the parts of something or the way it works.

4 What does the diagram on page 19 tell you? Discuss this with a partner.

Digital Learning

For a list of links and activities that relate to this Science standard, visit the California Treasures Web site at www.macmillanmh.com to access the Content Reader resources.

Have children view the Science in Motion video "Gravity at Work."

EL In addition, distribute copies of the Translated Concept Summaries in Spanish, Chinese, Hmong, Khmer, and Vietnamese.

Magnets Push and Pull

A magnet can push and pull. This is called magnetic force. A magnet can **attract**, or pull, objects made of iron. A magnet will not attract a penny because it is not made of iron. Is a quarter made of iron? How could you find out?

◀ This machine uses a very large magnet to pick up large objects.

Magnets can move things without even touching them. Magnets can pull through solids like paper, plastic, or glass. They can pull through liquids and gases, too. Every magnet has a magnetic field. This is the area around a magnet where its force pulls.

▼ A magnet will not attract objects made of brass, aluminum, or gold.

brass pot

aluminum can

gold ring

Magnets can pull through liquids and solids. ▶

Magnet-Powered Trains

What kind of train has no wheels and floats on air? Read on to find out!

Paul Souders/Corbis

The train is moving very fast. It is going 200 miles per hour (mph). The world outside its windows is a blur. Now the train is going 287 mph. At top speed it's going 310 mph. The passengers feel like they're on an amusement park ride. This is the world's fastest train. The train is in Shanghai, China. It takes people from the city center to the airport.

The trip takes 55 minutes in a car. In the world's fastest train, it takes less than 8 minutes. This train never touches the ground!

The train doesn't run on steel tracks. It doesn't have wheels. It doesn't even have a motor inside it. Its power comes from magnets! It is called a maglev train. The magnets are in a special track.

The track is called the guideway. Magnets in the guideway make the train move. They also guide it on its way. Magnets keep the train about a half inch off the track. Maglev trains are faster and quieter than other trains. They also use less energy.

How a Maglev Train Works

If you've ever played with magnets, you know they can push apart or pull together. Magnets pushing apart keep the maglev train up in the air. Powerful magnets in the guideway and on the train push the train up. An electric motor in the guideway creates a magnetic field. The magnetic field pulls the train along the guideway.

The world's only working maglev train is in Shanghai, China. Another maglev train in China is planned. It will connect Shanghai and Beijing. France, Germany, and the United States are very interested in maglev trains. —*Susan Moger*

▼ Shanghai, China, had the first working maglev train.

ChinaFotoPress/UPPA/ZUMA Press/Newscom

Description Writing Frame

Use the Writing Frame below to orally summarize "Magnets Push and Pull."

A magnet is _____

_____ .

This is called _____ .

A magnet can pull objects made _____ .

For example, a magnet will not attract a penny

because _____

_____ .

Magnets can pull through things **such as** _____

_____ .

Every magnet has a magnetic field, which is _____

_____ .

Use the frame to write the summary on another sheet of paper. Be sure to include the **bold** signal words. Keep this as a model of this Text Structure.

Critical Thinking

1   A magnet can _____, or pull, objects made of iron.

   A. attack

   B. push

   C. attract

2   Find the sentences in "Magnets Push and Pull" that tell what a magnet can do.

3   Point out the photograph in this article that shows how magnets work with liquids. What does the text explain about magnets and liquids?

4   What do the labels on page 25 name? Talk about these labels with a partner.

A label is a short word or phrase that describes someone or something.

Digital Learning

For a list of links and activities that relate to this Science standard, visit the California Treasures Web site at www.macmillanmh.com to access the Content Reader resources.

Have children view the e-Review "What Does a Magnet Pull?"

EL In addition, distribute copies of the Translated Concept Summaries in Spanish, Chinese, Hmong, Khmer, and Vietnamese.

What Is Sound?

Sound is made when something **vibrates**, or moves back and forth. When you snap a string, it vibrates. The air around it vibrates, too. This moving air goes to your ear. A part of your ear called the eardrum vibrates, and you hear sound.

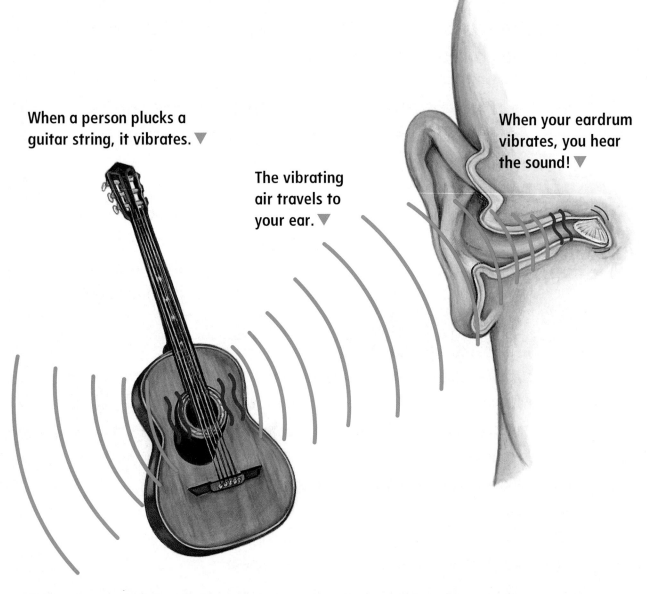

When a person plucks a guitar string, it vibrates. ▼

The vibrating air travels to your ear. ▼

When your eardrum vibrates, you hear the sound! ▼

When a sound is loud, the vibrations are big. When a sound is soft, the vibrations are small. When you yell, you make big vibrations. When you whisper, you make small vibrations. **Volume** describes the loudness of a sound.

Pitch describes how high or low a sound is. When a sound is low, the vibrations are slow. The moo of a cow has a low pitch. When a sound has a high pitch, the vibrations are fast. The meow of a cat has a high pitch.

high pitch   low pitch

◀ When you hit a small bar, the pitch is high. When you hit a big bar, the pitch is low.

Turn the Volume Down

Loud noises can hurt your ears, so turn down the sound!

Do you like to listen to music through headphones? If you do, turn down the volume. Loud sounds can hurt your hearing.

What is the loudest sound you ever heard? Thunder is loud. A fire truck's siren is loud too. You cannot control thunder or a fire siren. But you can control how loud some sounds are. When you turn up the volume on a TV or radio, the sound gets louder. When you turn down the volume, the sound gets quieter. When you have headphones on, turn down the volume.

Andy Caulfield/Getty Images

You hear sound when your eardrum vibrates. The vibration travels into other parts of your ear. Vibrations from loud sounds can hurt these parts. They can break or bend. If loud sounds continue, some parts of your ear may not get better. You may not be able to hear any more.

How long does it take for loud sounds to take away hearing? No one knows for sure. Some high school students already show signs of hearing loss. They didn't turn the volume down in time.

BananaStock/PunchStock

▲ Kids can hurt their ears if the music is too loud.

How Loud Is Too Loud?

Sound is measured in decibels. The chart shows how different sounds measure up. Sounds over 85 decibels can hurt your hearing.

Sound	Decibels
leaves moving on a tree	0
normal talking	50–60
alarm clock	80
chain saw	115
top volume on portable music player	115
jet engine	130

Problem/Solution Writing Frame

Use the Writing Frame below to orally summarize "Turn the Volume Down."

Parts of an ear can break or bend. This **problem** can happen when _____ .

The **solution** is to _____

_____ .

Headphones can be a **problem** if _____

_____ .

The **solution**? _____ .

No one knows for certain _____

_____ .

But some high school students already have a problem. They _____ .

Use the frame to write the summary on another sheet of paper. Be sure to include the **bold** signal words. Keep this as a model of this Text Structure.

Critical Thinking

1. When something moves back and forth, it_____.

    A. whispers

    B. volumes

    C. vibrates

2. Find the sentences in "What Is Sound?" that tell what happens when you snap a string.

3. Point out where this article describes pitch.

4. What happens first, next, and last in the diagram on page 30?

A diagram is a drawing or a plan. It explains the parts of something or the way it works.

Digital Learning

For a list of links and activities that relate to this Science standard, visit the California Treasures Web site at www.macmillanmh.com to access the Content Reader resources.

Have children view the e-Review "Sound."

EL In addition, distribute copies of the Translated Concept Summaries in Spanish, Chinese, Hmong, Khmer, and Vietnamese.

Plants and Their Parents

Cats have kittens and dogs have puppies. Animals have babies that look and act like their parents. Plants work the same way. A sunflower makes seeds that grow into sunflowers. An oak tree makes acorns that grow into oak trees. A **trait** is a way that a plant or animal looks or acts like its parents.

▲ A sunflower seed can grow into a sunflower.

Many characteristics that animals and plants get from their parents help the animals and plants to live in their environments. These characteristics, or traits, can include color, body parts, and sometimes how a plant or animal acts. For example, some animals have wings and can fly away from danger. Some cactuses that live in a dry desert have roots that do not grow deep. When it rains, these roots soak up water like a sponge.

▲ How does this tortoise stay safe?

▲ An acorn can grow into an oak tree.

Follow the Herd

Kevin Schafer/age fotostock/SuperStock

Special collars help protect elephants.

Lewis is a wild elephant. He lives in the Samburu National Reserve in Kenya, a country in Africa. Lewis spends his days as any elephant would. He eats, roams, and hangs out with his family. By doing what comes naturally, Lewis could help save his whole species—African elephants.

African elephants are endangered. That means the number of elephants is very low in some places. To protect them, there are nature reserves like Samburu. They give the animals a safe place to live.

But protecting animals as big as elephants can be hard. Elephants need a lot of food. They eat about 220 to 440 pounds of plants every day. It is hard to find spaces that are big enough and have enough food for them.

Linda Eberle/Alamy

◀ Zebras share Samburu with elephants.

Samburu is only 64 square miles. The elephants have to share that space with many other animals. Sometimes the elephants roam into areas that aren't safe.

Collecting the Clues

A group called the Save the Elephants Foundation is working to save the elephants. Scientists wanted to find out what makes elephants wander. Maybe then they could keep them safely in Samburu.

Save the Elephants put special collars around the necks of some elephants. Each collar had a special part on it. This part lets a satellite track the elephant.

Scientists learned that Lewis often left the reserve during the dry season. When there was little rain, he couldn't find enough to eat. He learned to find tasty crops at a farm.

This information will help Lewis. Scientists can give him food during the dry season. Then he and other elephants won't need to roam. —*Andrea Delbanco*

Claire Cerling

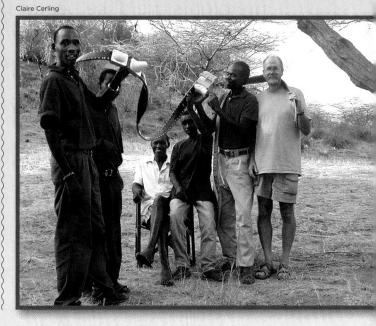

▲ The elephant collars are big!

Compare/Contrast Writing Frame

Use the Writing Frame below to orally summarize "Plants and Their Parents."

Animals and plants **both** have _____.

Sunflowers and oak trees are **different** plants, but sunflowers are **like** oak trees in that _____.

Plants and animals that live in the **same** environment can _____.

Some animals are **alike** in that they have _____

_____.

Some plants are **alike** because they have _____

_____.

So, **both** plants and animals have traits that _____

_____.

Use the frame to write the summary on another sheet of paper. Be sure to include the **bold** signal words. Keep this as a model of this Text Structure.

Critical Thinking

1 A way that a plant or an animal looks or acts like its parents is called a _____ .

    A. trait

    B. color

    C. tree

2 Compare and contrast the sunflower and oak tree in "Plants and Their Parents."

3 Revisit "Follow the Herd." Read aloud the text that tells what Lewis did during the dry season.

4 Which caption on page 37 is a question? Talk about an answer to this question with a partner.

A caption is text that goes along with a photograph or photographs.

Digital Learning

For a list of links and activities that relate to this Science standard, visit the California Treasures Web site at www.macmillanmh.com to access the Content Reader resources.

Have children view the e-Review "Animal Traits."

EL In addition, distribute copies of the Translated Concept Summaries in Spanish, Chinese, Hmong, Khmer, and Vietnamese.

A Butterfly's Life

Butterflies lay eggs on leaves and branches. Some butterflies lay many eggs in one spot. Other butterflies lay each egg in a different spot. But after ten days, a caterpillar comes out of each egg. The caterpillar eats leaves and grows.

butterfly egg

caterpillar

A Frog's Life

frog eggs

tadpole

Every spring a male frog starts calling to find a mate. After he finds her, the female frog lays eggs in water. They look like balls of jelly with dark spots.

Tadpoles hatch from these eggs. They use their tails to swim. They eat plants and grow bigger.

42

After three weeks, the caterpillar forms a hard case around itself. This is the **pupa**. Inside the pupa the caterpillar changes into a butterfly. When the butterfly is fully grown, it crawls out of the pupa.

pupa   **young butterfly**   **adult butterfly**

young frog

After a while, each tadpole grows legs. Its tail shrinks. A young frog begins to move onto land.

adult frog

Finally, the young frog hops out of the water. Its tail is gone. It is an adult frog.

Monarchs on the Move

Monarch butterflies eat, grow, and fly away.

Have you ever seen butterflies like these fluttering through the air? Every August, millions of monarch butterflies begin a long trip. They fly from the cold north to spend the winter in the warm south. Some fly 2,000 miles. A monarch can fly 100 miles in one day!

Monarchs spend the winter sleeping. Large groups hang together on trees in warm places like Mexico. In the spring the monarchs fly north again. When they get where they're going, the females lay eggs. Late in the summer the butterflies from those eggs head south.

Patricio Robles Gil/Sierra Madre/Minden Pictures/Getty Images

From Egg to Caterpillar to Butterfly

Michael Hood/Alamy

Don Johnston/Alamy

When a monarch butterfly egg hatches, a caterpillar comes out. Its job is to eat and grow. When it grows up, it will look very different.

The caterpillar changes into a beautiful butterfly!

Bob Sciarrino/Star Ledger/Corbis

Danny Lehman/CORBIS

Soon it is time to fly. Monarchs have very strong wings. They can fly for hours without stopping. There's a long trip ahead.

Now it's time to rest. The long trip is over. These monarchs will rest in Mexico all winter long.

Sequence Writing Frame

Use the Writing Frame below to orally summarize "A Frog's Life."

Every spring a male frog finds a female frog.

After he finds her, _____

_____ .

Next the tadpoles hatch. **Then** they _____

_____ .

After a while, each tadpole _____

_____ .

Finally, _____

_____ .

Use the frame to write the summary on another sheet of paper. Use this model to write another summary for "A Butterfly's Life." Be sure to include the **bold** signal words. Keep this as a model of this Text Structure.

Critical Thinking

1 The hard case that the caterpillar forms around itself is called the _____ .

    A. tadpole

    B. pupa

    C. butterfly

2 Find the text in "Monarchs on the Move" that tells what happens after a butterfly egg hatches.

3 Read aloud the text in this article that talks about what happens after the caterpillar changes into a butterfly.

4 Use the diagram on pages 42 and 43 to talk with a partner about how a butterfly grows and changes.

A diagram is a drawing or a plan. It explains the parts of something or the way it works.

Digital Learning

For a list of links and activities that relate to this Science standard, visit the California Treasures Web site at www.macmillanmh.com to access the Content Reader resources. Have children view the Science in Motion video "Crab Life Cycle."

EL In addition, distribute copies of the Translated Concept Summaries in Spanish, Chinese, Hmong, Khmer, and Vietnamese.

The Life Cycle of Black Bears

In January or February, one to five black bears may be born to a mother bear. By spring, the cubs weigh about ten pounds each. They are big enough to explore the environment with their mother. They learn how to get food and survive.

▲ These young black bear cubs will learn how to survive.

When the cubs are a year old, they are ready to leave their mother and be on their own.

Bears have their own cubs when they become between three and four years of age. Bears live to be between twelve and fifteen years old.

▲ This black bear is an adult.

▲ Some black bears in Alaska have light fur that helps them hide in the snow.

What Is a Population?

A **population** is a group of the same kind of animal that lives near each other. For example, the black bears that live in Yosemite National Park are one population. The black bears that live in Canada are another population. They share traits such as fur, four legs, and claws.

Since animal populations live in different places, they may be different from each other. This can be because of the environment. For example, some black bear populations have light fur that helps them hide in the snow.

Daddy Day Care

Baboon fathers help take care of their babies.

Scientists have learned something surprising about baboons. Some baboon fathers help mother baboons care for their babies. Part of the surprise was that male baboons can tell which babies are theirs.

Scientists used tests to match 75 baboon babies with their fathers. Half of these fathers spent time with their babies until the babies were three years old. Male baboons can be fierce fighters.

"But they can be sweet with infants," says Joan Silk, one of the scientists. The fathers rush in if one of their babies is in danger.

The scientists think baboon fathers know their babies by sight and by smell. "It's always fun to find out that animals are smarter than you thought!" says Silk. —*Elizabeth Winchester*

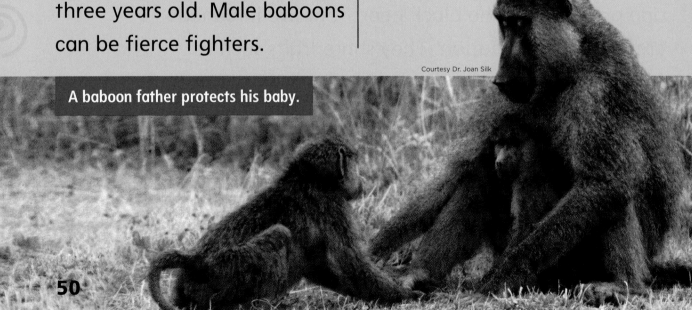

Courtesy Dr. Joan Silk

A baboon father protects his baby.

Good Dads

Baboons aren't the only proud fathers in the animal world. Here are some other examples of animal dads that care for their kids.

Tim Davis/Corbis

Michael & Patricia Fogden/Minden Pictures/Getty Images

Darwin's Frog This frog father carries up to 15 eggs inside a special part of his throat. After the eggs hatch and the tadpoles have turned into frogs, they hop out.

Emperor Penguin A penguin pop balances the mother's egg on his feet. He uses his skin and feathers to protect the egg from the bitter cold. He does this for nine weeks, without eating, until the egg is ready to hatch.

Leszczynski, Zigmund/Animals Animals

Sea Horse A female sea horse lays her eggs in a pouch in the front of the male's stomach. The male sea horse carries the eggs until they hatch. When the babies are big enough, they swim away.

Description Writing Frame

Use the Writing Frame below to orally summarize "What Is a Population?"

A population is a group of the same kind of animals that often live near each other. **For example,** _____

_____.

The bears that live in Yosemite National Park are all black bears, **so** they _____

_____.

For instance, _____

_____.

However, animal populations may be different from each other. **For example,** _____

_____.

Use the frame to write the summary on another sheet of paper. Be sure to include the **bold** signal words. Keep this as a model of this Text Structure.

Critical Thinking

1. A group of the same kind of animals that live near each other is called a _____.

   A. bear

   B. national park

   C. population

2. Point to the text in "Daddy Day Care" that tells how baboon fathers might know their babies.

3. Which sentence in "The Life Cycle of Black Bears" tells how much cubs weigh by spring?

4. Read aloud the caption that describes an adult bear.

> A caption is a title or an explanation of a photograph

Digital Learning

For a list of links and activities that relate to this Science standard, visit the California Treasures Web site at www.macmillanmh.com to access the Content Reader resources.

Have children view the e-Review, "Animal Traits."

EL In addition, distribute copies of the Translated Concept Summaries in Spanish, Chinese, Hmong, Khmer, and Vietnamese.

How Plants Change to Get What They Need

Plants need light to grow. The stems and leaves and flowers of a plant will even move to get more light. They will grow toward light.

Many plants also need soil to grow. They take in food and water from the soil.

▲ This plant bends toward the light that comes through the window.

Some flowers will follow the Sun as it moves across the sky during the day. ▼

Plants begin as seeds. When a seed **germinates**, it begins to grow. When plants grow, the roots push down toward Earth. Gravity helps. Gravity is a force given off by Earth. Gravity pulls things on or near Earth's surface toward the center of the planet.

Some plants have to change to stay safe when the environment changes. As a pumpkin grows, its vines will climb around things that it touches. This helps the plant get light. On a coast, the wind can be so strong that all the branches on the trees bend. The branches grow behind the trunk because it protects them from the wind.

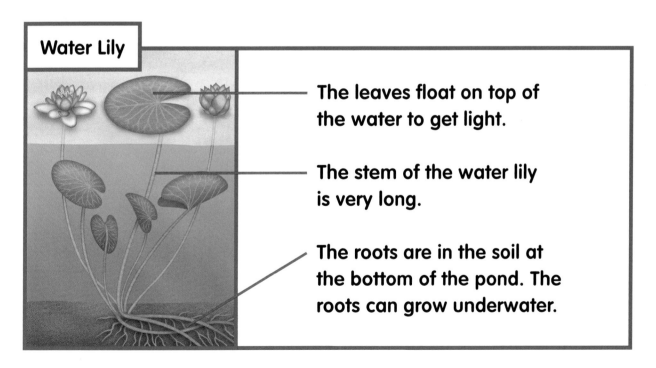

Water Lily

The leaves float on top of the water to get light.

The stem of the water lily is very long.

The roots are in the soil at the bottom of the pond. The roots can grow underwater.

From Seed to Fruit

These steps show how a pumpkin grows.

Start with Seeds

Seeds go into the soil.
Sunny spots are best.
Sun helps pumpkins grow.

IT Stock Free/Jupiter Images

Next Come the Sprouts

Small sprouts come up from the soil. Water and sunlight help them grow bigger.

Shmuel Thaler/Index Stock

Leaves and Flowers

Weeks pass. Leaves grow on the pumpkin vines. Then come flowers. One flower opens at a time.

Ingram Publishing/SuperStock

Green Pumpkins

Fruits grow on the vines. They are tiny at first. Each fruit stays green for months. The pumpkins are not yet ripe.

AP Photo/Port Huron Times Herald, J. Douglas Brooks

Orange Pumpkins

The fruits take in warmth, water, and sunlight. Each one grows big and orange. Now the pumpkins are ripe!

RVN/Alamy

Top 5 Pumpkin-Producing States

Every fall, pumpkin patches get loads of visitors who come to pick out pumpkins. One year, these states grew the most pumpkins.

1. **Illinois,** 299 million pounds
2. **California,** 150 million
3. **Pennsylvania,** 117 million
4. **New York,** 107 million
5. **Michigan,** 60 million

Andy Caulfield/Getty Images

57

Cause/Effect Writing Frame

Use the Writing Frame below to orally summarize "How Plants Change to Get What They Need."

There are many things that can affect the growth and development of plants.

Plants need _____

_____ .

When plants get this, the **effect** is _____

_____ .

Many plants also need _____

_____ **because** _____

_____ .

When the environment changes, _____

_____ .

This can **affect** _____ .

Use the frame to write the summary on another sheet of paper. Be sure to include the **bold** signal words. Keep this as a model of this Text Structure.

Critical Thinking

1 When a seed germinates, it begins to _____.

   A. green

   B. grow

   C. die

2 Find the text in "From Seed to Fruit" that tells what helps pumpkins grow.

3 Point to the text in "From Seed to Fruit" that describes what grows first on pumpkin vines.

4 Discuss the diagram on page 55 with a partner. Why do you think the stem of the water lily is long?

A diagram is a drawing or a plan. It explains the parts of something or the way it works.

Digital Learning

For a list of links and activities that relate to this Science standard, visit the California Treasures Web site at www.macmillanmh.com to access the Content Reader resources.

Have children view the Science in Motion video "Life Cycle of A Pine Tree."

EL In addition, distribute copies of the translated concept summaries in Spanish, Chinese, Hmong, Khmer, and Vietnamese.

What Do Flowers, Fruits, and Seeds Do?

Many plants have flowers. Flowers come in different colors, shapes, and sizes. Even though they look different, all flowers make seeds. Some plants that have flowers also make **fruit**. Most of the time, the seed or seeds grow inside the fruit. The fruit keeps the seeds safe and helps them grow. Some fruits, like strawberries, have the seeds on the outside. Other fruits, like apples and blueberries, have seeds on the inside.

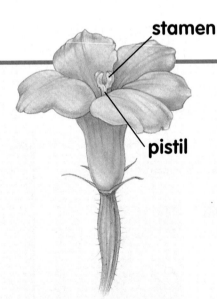

stamen

pistil

Pollen moves from the stamen to the pistil. Then the flower starts to change.

The flower grows bigger and the petals fall off. It grows into a fruit.

The fruit protects the seeds inside.

Flowers have special parts so they can make new plants. The **stamen** of the flower makes pollen, a sticky powder. The **pistil** takes in the **pollen** and makes seeds. The seeds can grow into new plants.

Sometimes birds and bees move pollen from a stamen to a pistil. But wind and water can move pollen too. When the pollen lands on the pistil, the flower starts to lose its petals. The flower begins to grow into fruit with seeds.

The seeds inside the fruit can grow into new plants.

After the fruit is ripe, it falls to the ground.

Bees, Bats, Bears, and Bison

What could these animals possibly have in common? Hint: It's about plants!

A bee buzzes. A bat flies at night. A bear walks through a forest. A bison grazes. These animals are very different, but they have one thing in common. They are part of the process of growing plants.

Seeds Start with Pollen

Plants grow from seeds. The seeds come from pollen. The pollen and seeds are made in the plant's flowers.

To make seeds, pollen has to move from one part of the plant to another. Pollen also moves from plant to plant. How does pollen get from one place to another? Sometimes bees and bats carry it. Bees and bats fly to flowers to get food. They fly from flower to flower. Along the way, they touch pollen. Pollen sticks to their bodies. When the bee or bat moves to a new flower, pollen rubs off. Then the plant can make seeds.

Plants Start from Seeds

A seed needs soil to grow. How do seeds get from the plant to the soil? Sometimes bats, bears, and bison help out.

A bear finds a blueberry patch. A fruit-eating bat lands in a banana tree. A bison chews tall grass. When these animals eat fruit and grass, they are also eating seeds. The seeds go in with the food. Later they come out in the animal's droppings. The seeds in the droppings grow into plants.

Westend 61/Alamy

Sometimes seeds stick to the fur of bears and bison. When those animals lie down, the seeds come off on the ground. A new plant can grow there.

Plants grow from the seeds. Flowers grow on plants. Flowers make pollen. Pollen makes seeds. Hungry bees, bats, bears, and bison go looking for food. Now it starts all over again! —*Susan Moger*

First Light/Getty Images

Compare/Contrast Writing Frame

Use the Writing Frame below to orally summarize "What Do Flowers, Fruits, and Seeds Do?"

Many plants have flowers, **but** _____

_____ .

Even though the flowers look **different**, they are

alike in that _____

_____ .

Some flowers **also** make fruit. Most of the time,

the fruit _____ .

This is true with _____

_____ .

However, some fruits, such as strawberries,

_____ .

Use the frame to write the summary on another
sheet of paper. Be sure to include the **bold** signal
words. Keep this as a model of this Text Structure.

Critical Thinking

1 Pollen is made by a flower's _____.

    A. strawberry

    B. stamen

    C. cantaloupe

2 Which parts of the text in "Bees, Bats, Bears, and Bison" explain how animals help plants?

3 Point to the text in this article that talks about how seeds get from a plant to the soil.

4 Use the diagram on pages 60 and 61 to talk about how a flower grows and changes into a cantaloupe.

A diagram is a drawing or a plan. It explains the parts of something or the way it works.

Digital Learning

For a list of links and activities that relate to this Science standard, visit the California Treasures Web site at www.macmillanmh.com to access the Content Reader resources.

Have children view the e-Review "Plants Grow and Change."

EL In addition, distribute copies of the Translated Concept Summaries in Spanish, Chinese, Hmong, Khmer, and Vietnamese.

What Are Rocks Made Of?

All rocks are made of **minerals**. Some rocks are made of just one mineral. Other rocks are made of many minerals.

Look at the piece of granite. It is made of three minerals. The white parts are the mineral feldspar. The gray parts are quartz. The black parts are mica.

▲ Beryl is made of only one mineral.

Minerals in Granite

quartz

feldspar

mica

Did you know that you use minerals every day? Your pencil is made of the mineral graphite. Plants use the minerals in soil to help them grow. Our bodies need minerals, too. We get minerals from the foods we eat.

▼fluorite

▲ Some toothpastes have fluoride, which is made from the mineral fluorite.

MONUMENTAL MATERIAL

Different kinds of rock are good for making monuments.

Some monuments are made by people. Some are part of nature. This is the story of three famous monuments. —*Susan Moger*

Mount Rushmore

Mount Rushmore is in South Dakota. People carved this monument to honor four presidents of the United States. Their faces are carved into a single rock of granite. Each face is 60 feet tall.

The granite in Mount Rushmore is very hard. It wears away very slowly. This monument should be around for a long time.

Digital Vision/Getty Images

The Lincoln Memorial

The Lincoln Memorial honors President Abraham Lincoln. It was carved from white marble from Georgia. Marble is very hard. It can be polished to make it smooth and shiny.

Other parts of the monument are made of Indiana limestone and Massachusetts granite.

IN THIS TEMPLE
AS IN THE HEARTS OF THE PEOPLE
FOR WHOM HE SAVED THE UNION
THE MEMORY OF ABRAHAM LINCOLN
IS ENSHRINED FOREVER

BananaStock/Punchstock

The Grand Canyon

The Grand Canyon is a natural monument. It was carved out of rock by the Colorado River. It started 6 million years ago, and the river is still carving.

The canyon has many kinds of rocks. The river and wind wear down these rocks in different ways. These differences give the Grand Canyon its interesting shape.

Jen Judge/Getty Images

Compare/Contrast Writing Frame

Use the Writing Frame below to orally summarize "What Are Rocks Made Of?"

Some rocks are made of one mineral, **but** _____

_____ .

Beryl and granite are **both** _____ ,

but beryl _____ .

Granite, **on the other hand,** is _____

_____ .

People use minerals every day. Some people _____

_____ ,

while other people _____ .

Both plants and people _____ .

Use the frame to write the summary on another sheet of paper. Be sure to include the **bold** signal words. Keep this as a model of this Text Structure.

Critical Thinking

1. All rocks are made of _____.

   A. minerals

   B. pencils

   C. beryl

2. Read aloud the name of the monument in "Monumental Material" that honors four presidents.

3. Point out the text in this article that describes the statue of Abraham Lincoln.

4. Use the diagram on page 66 to talk about what minerals are in granite.

A diagram is a drawing or a plan that explains the parts of something or how it works.

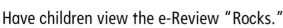

Digital Learning

For a list of links and activities that relate to this Science standard, visit the California Treasures Web site at www.macmillanmh.com to access the Content Reader resources.

Have children view the e-Review "Rocks."

EL In addition, distribute copies of the Translated Concept Summaries in Spanish, Chinese, Hmong, Khmer, and Vietnamese.

How Do Rocks Change?

Did you know that rocks can change size and shape? The way water and wind change rocks is called **weathering**. When water gets into the cracks of rocks, it can freeze and push against them. The cracks get bigger and the rocks break. And when rocks slide down a hill, they may break and become smaller. Smaller rocks can break down into sand. Tiny rocks can become part of the soil.

▼ Strong winds can blow sand against rocks.
  Wind and sand wore this rock into an arch.

Weathering is not the only thing that causes rocks to change. Earthquakes can change rocks, too. When Earth shakes, rocks rub against each other. They can break into smaller pieces.

Plants can also change rocks. Plants can grow in soil inside the cracks of rocks. Sometimes the roots are so strong, they cause the rocks to break.

The roots of this tree have grown into the rock and cracked it. ▶

Secret Life of Rocks

Igneous rocks start out as magma from deep inside Earth.

You may think a rock is always just a rock. Maybe this will change your mind.

Rocks are not alive the way people, plants, and animals are. But all rocks have a beginning. Some arrive on Earth's surface in a burst of fire. Some are made from millions of animal skeletons. Some change from one kind of rock to another.

The Story of a Rock

Suppose a scientist picks up a rock. It is granite, a very hard rock. Here's a story the scientist might tell.

Granite is an igneous rock. Igneous means "of fire." So the first chapter in granite's story is about magma. Magma is melted rock deep inside Earth. Magma is always moving. Sometimes it forces its way up close to Earth's crust.

In the second chapter, magma near Earth's crust stops moving. It cools down. It becomes as solid as a rock! This rock is granite. It is still covered by Earth's crust.

The next chapter covers millions of years. As Earth's crust wears away, the granite shows through. The rock wears down. Maybe a glacier scrapes across it. Wind blows sand at it. Rain pours on it. Water gets into a crack in the rock. When the water freezes, it breaks the rock apart.

Connie Coleman/Getty Images

The End

Rocks do not die. But they can be chipped away and broken down by water and wind. They bump other rocks. That wears them down, too. Rocks get smaller and smaller. Some end up as grains of sand. Sand is a sediment. In time, layers of sediment become sedimentary rock. The cycle goes on.

Jim Lundgren/Alamy

Michael Szoenyi/Photo Researchers

This Planet Rocks

Earth is the largest rocky planet we know of. Mars is also rocky, but it is smaller. Earth has a thin rocky crust. If Earth were the size a tomato, the crust would be as thick as a tomato's skin.

Cause/Effect Writing Frame

Use the Writing Frame below to orally summarize "How Do Rocks Change?"

If water gets into the cracks of rocks, **then** _____

_____.

This can **cause** _____.

Rocks can become smaller **as a result of** _____

_____, **because** _____.

Sand is the **effect of** _____

_____.

Earthquakes can **cause** rocks to change **because** _____

_____.

Therefore, we know that _____

_____.

Use the frame to write the summary on another sheet of paper. Be sure to include the **bold** signal words. Keep it as a model of this Text Structure.

Critical Thinking

1 The way water and wind change rocks is called _____.

    A. sand

    B. weathering

    C. water

2 Revisit the text on page 74. Find the sentence that tells what *igneous* means.

3 Run your finger under the sentence in "Secret Life of Rocks" that tells what eventually happens to rocks.

4 Does the caption on page 72 or 73 describe what strong winds can do to a rock? Ask a partner to point to the photograph that goes with this caption.

A caption is a title or an explanation of a photograph.

Digital Learning

For a list of links and activities that relate to this Science standard, visit the California Treasures Web site at www.macmillanmh.com to access the Content Reader resources.

Science

Have children view the Science e-Review "Rocks Change."

EL In addition, distribute copies of the translated concept summaries in Spanish, Chinese, Hmong, Khmer, and Vietnamese.

What Is Soil?

Soil is made up of tiny rocks and bits of plants and animals. Rocks break down and become part of the soil, too. Plants and animals die and rot. They also break down into the soil.

Most plants grow in soil. They take in minerals from it. When people and animals eat plants, they get the minerals that they need.

▼ Sandy soil is light brown. This kind of soil does not hold much water.

There are many kinds of soil. Some soils are red, others are brown or black. The minerals in the soils give them their colors. Most plants grow best in topsoil because it has many nutrients.

◀ Clay soil gets its red color from iron. Clay soil does not take in much water.

◀ Topsoil is dark brown or black. It has bits of dead animals and plants in it. Topsoil can hold a lot of water.

A Martian Garden

Can vegetables grow in Martian soil on Earth?

Michael Mautner is a scientist and a gardener. He had an idea. He wanted to know if he could grow vegetables here on Earth in soil from Mars.

G. Brad Lewis/Getty Images

▲ **Could Earth vegetables grow in Martian soil?**

Martian Rocks Hit Earth

Mautner did not go to Mars to get the soil. He made it from Martian rocks that were already here. The rocks from Mars fell through space. They landed on Earth. Space rocks that land on Earth are called meteorites. A lot of meteorites hit Earth. Not many of them come from Mars. Mautner proved that his did. One Martian rock was found in the Sahara Desert. The other was found in Antarctica. Both are good places for spotting space rocks.

▼ **A meteorite from Mars**

AFP/Newscom

80

In the Mix

Mautner took slices from the Martian rocks. He found chemicals inside them. These same chemicals on Earth are used in fertilizer. Fertilizer helps plants grow.

Mautner ground up the slices of Martian rock to make soil. This soil had the fertilizer chemicals in it.

Mautner mixed the Martian soil with water. Then he put pieces of asparagus and potatoes in the mixture. In a few weeks the plants grew a couple of inches tall. These plants were healthy. He grew other plants in plain water. He also grew some in water mixed with other ground-up rocks. These test plants were smaller. They were not as healthy as the plants grown in Martian soil.

Mautner says, "In the future, people starting a colony on Mars could use the soil there to grow food." —*Susan Moger*

Courtesy Michael Mautner

▲ A tiny asparagus plant sprouts in Martian soil mixed with water.

Skip Jeffery

▲ The asparagus plant grows bigger!

Phil Marden

Cause/Effect Writing Frame

Use the Writing Frame below to orally summarize "What Is Soil?"

When rocks break down into tiny pieces, **then** they

_____.

When plants and animals die and rot, **then** _____

_____.

Most plants get their minerals from soil. **Therefore**

_____.

Because the minerals in soils give them their colors,

_____.

Therefore, we know that _____

_____.

Use the frame to write the summary on another sheet of paper. Be sure to include the **bold** signal words. Keep this as a model of this Text Structure.

Critical Thinking

1　Tiny rocks and bits of plants and animals make up _____.

　　A. sand

　　B. soil

　　C. minerals

2　Find the text in "A Martian Garden" that tells how Michael Mautner got soil from Mars.

3　Point out the sentences in "A Martian Garden" that tell about what Mautner did.

4　Discuss with a partner the captions on pages 78 and 79. Describe each kind of soil.

A caption is a title or an explanation of a photograph.

Digital Learning

For a list of links and activities that relate to this Science standard, visit the California Treasures Web site at www.macmillanmh.com to access the Content Reader resources.

Have children view the Science e-Review "Soils."

EL In addition, distribute copies of the translated concept summaries in Spanish, Chinese, Hmong, Khmer, and Vietnamese.

What Are Fossils?

A **fossil** is what is left of a living thing from the past. Scientists find fossils of plants and animals in rock, ice, tar, or amber. Amber is a sticky liquid from trees that has become hard. It can contain trapped plants and bugs. Scientists study fossils because they are evidence of the plants and animals that lived long ago.

▲ This insect got trapped in amber millions of years ago.

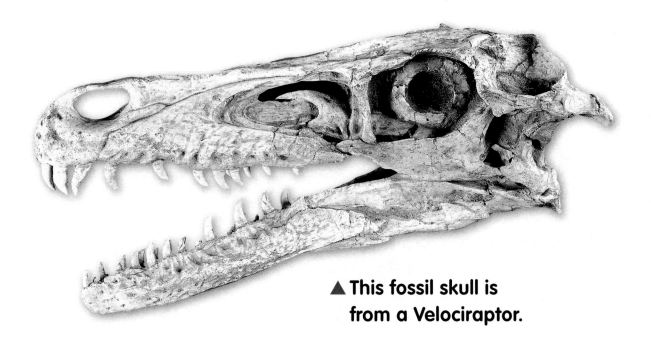

▲ This fossil skull is from a Velociraptor.

This fish fossil was found in a dry place in Wyoming.

Fossils give clues about the history of Earth. Animal fossils tell what kinds of animals roamed here long ago. Plant and animal fossils tell what the land might have looked like many years back. For example, by studying fossils, scientists have learned that the weather was different millions of years ago. In Antarctica, scientists found fossils of plants that only grow in warm places today. So the scientists infer that the weather in Antarctica used to be warm.

Found: A Rain Forest in Illinois

How do we know that there was once a rain forest in Illinois?

Rain forests are tropical forests. That means they are located in hot parts of the world. Most of them are near the equator. From the name *rain forest*, you can tell that they get a lot of rain.

Illinois is a state in the part of the United States called the Midwest. It is not near the equator. But 300 million years ago a rain forest grew there. How do we know? Scientists found fossils of trees and plants. They were once part of a rain forest.

Today, most rain forests grow near the equator, far from Illinois. ▶

Digital Vision

AP Photo/The Illinois State Geological Survey

This fossil of an ancient rain forest plant was found in an Illinois coal mine.

A Forest of Fossils

A fossil is the remains of something that lived long ago. Fossils are usually found as parts of rocks. The plants in the Illinois rain forest were buried in mud 300 million years ago. Over millions of years the mud became rock. The plants became fossils.

The rain forest is buried 200 feet underground. Coal miners dug down that deep. John Nelson, a scientist who studies rocks, was the first person to find the fossils. Scientists have now found a whole forest. There are fossils of trees, mosses, ferns, and other plants. Some of the ferns are 12 feet tall.

What Was the Rain Forest Like?

The plants in the Illinois rain forest were bigger than plants today. The rain forest was very hot and humid. Humid means the air feels wet even when it isn't raining. There were animals in the rain forest. But their fossils have not been found.

The fossils show us what the rain forest plants looked like the day mud covered them. "It's a snapshot in time," said one of the scientists. —*Susan Moger*

Description Writing Frame

Use the Writing Frame below to orally summarize "What Are Fossils?"

Scientists have found many fossils of _____

_____.

Fossils can be found in places **such as** _____

_____.

Fossils give clues about the history of Earth. **For instance,**

_____.

Fossils tell what the land might have looked like many

years back. **For example,** _____

_____.

In Antarctica, **for instance,** _____.

This told scientists that _____.

Use the frame to write the summary on another
sheet of paper. Be sure to include the **bold** signal
words. Keep this as a model of this Text Structure.

Critical Thinking

1 Something that is left of a living thing from the past is called _____.

    A. a fossil

    B. a fish

    C. amber

2 Point out the sentence in "Found: A Rain Forest in Illinois" that tells what rain forests are.

3 With a partner, discuss what the article says about fossils.

4 Describe for a partner the photograph of the velociraptor fossil on page 84.

A photograph is a picture taken with a camera.

Digital Learning

For a list of links and activities that relate to this Science standard, visit the California Treasures Web site at www.macmillanmh.com to access the Content Reader resources.

Have children view the Science in Motion video "How A Fossil Forms."

EL In addition, distribute copies of the Translated Concept Summaries in Spanish, Chinese, Hmong, Kmer, and Vietnamese.

How We Use Natural Resources

A **natural resource** is something from Earth that people use. Rocks, minerals, plants, soil, and water are resources from Earth that people use. These natural resources are used to make many things. Your shirt might be made from the cotton of a plant. Your desk might be made out of wood.

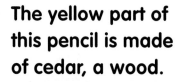

The eraser is made from the sap of a rubber tree.

The yellow part of this pencil is made of cedar, a wood.

The gray part is made of graphite, a mineral.

Rocks are often used to build homes. Concrete is made by mixing rocks, sand, and water. It is used to make buildings and sidewalks. Salt is also a natural resource—it is a mineral. Have you ever put salt on your food?

▲ **Salt is a mineral that we eat.**

Water is a natural resource that we drink, cook with and clean with. Water is also used to grow food. We use moving water to make electrical power that gives us light and heats homes. Like water, wind can also make electrical power.

▼ **The water that moves over the dam has a lot of force. We can use this force.**

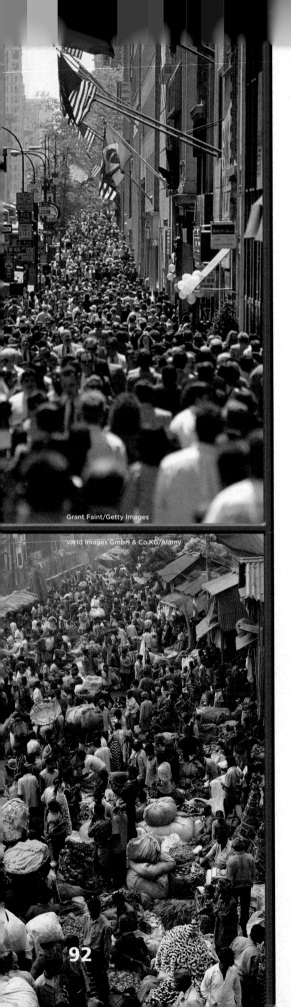

Grant Faint/Getty Images

vario images GmbH & Co.KG/Alamy

It's Getting Crowded Around Here!

A lot of people have to share Earth's resources.

Blink your eyes. In that time, three people were born. Blink again. That's another three people! Every minute there are 184 more people. Every hour there are 11,040 more. Every day 264,960 people are added to the total. That makes 97 million more people on Earth every year.

By 2007 the total number of people on Earth was six and a half billion. A stack of 6 billion pennies would be 5,000 miles high!

Growing Pains

Earth has a limited supply of some things every person needs. Take water, for example. Water covers most of the planet. But less than 1 percent of it can be used for drinking and washing. One of every 13 people around the world does not have enough clean water.

Food is a problem too. One of every 7 people in the world does not get enough to eat. Why? As cities grow bigger, farmland disappears. Buildings and roads take its place. There is less room to grow food, and there are more people to feed.

Every person alive uses Earth's supplies. Some use more than others. Using less and wasting less are keys to a good future.

Making Sure There's Enough to Go Around

Can six and a half billion people figure out how to share and save Earth's resources? Bill Ryan of the United Nations thinks so. He believes young people will change the world. "There are more young people alive now than at any other time," he says.

Stockbyte/Getty Images

Element

Top 5 Countries with the Largest Populations

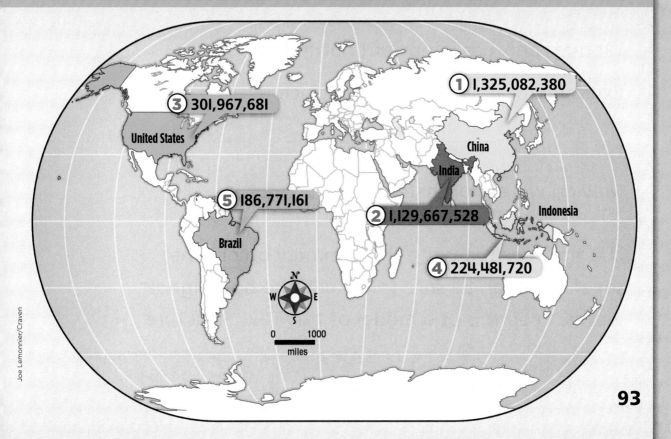

③ 301,967,681
United States

① 1,325,082,380
China

India

② 1,129,667,528

Indonesia

④ 224,481,720

⑤ 186,771,161
Brazil

N
W E
S
0   1000
miles

Joe Lemonnier/Craven

Description Writing Frame

Use the Writing Frame below to orally summarize "How We Use Natural Resources."

Natural resources have **many interesting qualities** and are used _____.

For example, your shirt might be _____

_____.

Or, **for instance**, your _____.

Rocks are natural resources that _____

_____.

Water is another important natural resource.

Examples of how we use water include _____

_____.

Moving water, **for instance**, _____.

Use the frame to write the summary on another sheet of paper. Be sure to include the **bold** signal words. Keep this as a model of this Text Structure.

Critical Thinking

1   Something from Earth that people use is called a _____ .

    A. new home

    B. lot of force

    C. natural resource

2   Point to the sentence in "It's Getting Crowded Around Here!" that tells how much water can be used for drinking and washing.

3   Where in this article can you find information about food?

A diagram is a drawing or a plan. It explains the parts of something or the way it works.

4   Explain the diagram on page 90 to a partner.

Digital Learning

For a list of links and activities that relate to this Science standard, visit the California Treasures Web site at www.macmillanmh.com to access the Content Reader resources.

Have children view the e-Review "Natural Resources."

EL In addition, distribute copies of the Translated Concept Summaries in Spanish, Chinese, Hmong, Khmer, and Vietnamese.

Then and Now

Tamika wanted to learn about her **ancestors**. Ancestors are family members who lived long ago. So Tamika interviewed her grandmother. She told Tamika about her ancestors who lived in Nigeria, a country in Africa. They wore brightly colored shirts called *bubas*. A woman wore a scarf called a *gele*. Tamika's grandmother had a gele to show her.

▼ Photographs can help people trace their families through history.

96

Tamika's grandmother told her of how their ancestors moved to the United States many years ago. They lived and worked on a farm. They got eggs to eat from chickens and milk from cows.

When Tamika's grandmother was a girl, a milkman delivered eggs and milk to her home. Today Tamika and her family go to a store to buy milk, eggs, and other groceries. When they get home, Tamika puts the eggs and milk into the refrigerator the way her grandmother did when she was Tamika's age.

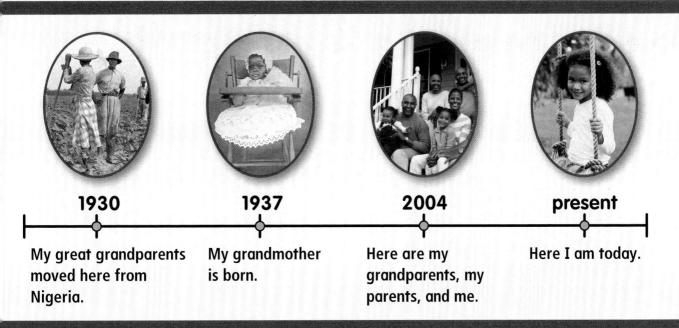

1930	1937	2004	present
My great grandparents moved here from Nigeria.	My grandmother is born.	Here are my grandparents, my parents, and me.	Here I am today.

▲ By gathering information, Tamika was able to make a time line of her family's history.

Same Place, Different Times!

Take a look at how one California city has changed.

Recently, Freddy Gartz discovered a large book in the attic of his house in Anaheim, California. The book was a photo album. The seven-year-old showed it to his father and grandfather.

Many photos were of fields and orange groves. "I took these pictures of Anaheim in the 1940s and 1950s," said his grandfather.

▼ Anaheim used to have many farms and orange groves.

In those days, Anaheim was a small city with few big buildings. Most of it was farmland for oranges.

Freddy was surprised. Today, Anaheim is a big city with tall buildings. The farmland has been covered. The orange trees are gone.

Freddy's father explained why. He said in the 1950s a huge theme park was built in Anaheim. A road was built to connect Los Angeles and Anaheim.

▼ Today Anaheim is a busy city.

Tony Freeman/PhotoEdit Inc.

Courtesy of Anaheim Public Library

The road made it easier to get to Anaheim. Businesses and workers started coming. The city got larger and larger. Soon, most of the orange trees were cut down to make way for houses.

Liane Cary/SuperStock

Today Anaheim is the tenth-biggest city in California.

Freddy wondered what his grandfather did for fun as a kid. "We mostly listened to the radio," said his grandfather.

Freddy's father said there was no TV until the 1950s. Back then, TV was in black and white.

Bettmann/Corbis

Freddy couldn't imagine what it would be like without color TV, CD players, computers, and video games.

Freddy's father pointed out that there is more to do in Anaheim now. There are baseball teams and hockey teams, concert halls and shopping centers.

What else did Freddy discover that day? Things change over time. —*Curtis Slepian*

ONOKY - Photononstop/Alamy

Sequence Writing Frame

Use the Writing Frame below to orally summarize "Then and Now."

Tamika wanted to learn about her family members from long ago.

First, she _____

_____ .

To begin, Tamika's grandmother told her _____

_____ .

Next, Tamika's grandmother _____

_____ .

After that, they _____

_____ .

Use the frame to write the summary on another sheet of paper. Be sure to include the **bold** signal words. Keep this as a model of this Text Structure.

Critical Thinking

1   Your family members that lived long ago are called your _____.

    A. ancestors

    B. friends

    C. bubas

2   Point to the sentence in "Same Place, Different Times!" that tells when Anaheim was mostly open fields and farmland.

3   Read aloud the sentence that tells what Freddy's grandfather did for fun when he was a kid.

4   Use the time line to find out when Tamika's grandmother was born.

A time line shows important events in the order in which they happened.

Digital Learning

For a list of links and activities that relate to this History/ Social Science standard, visit the California Treasures Web site at www.macmillanmh.com to access the Content Reader resources.

Have children view the video "Families Long Ago."

All About Location

Look at the things in this classroom photo. Each thing is in a certain place, or location. A location is the place or area where something is. The work table is located in the bottom right of the photo. The globe is located on the cubbies by the door.

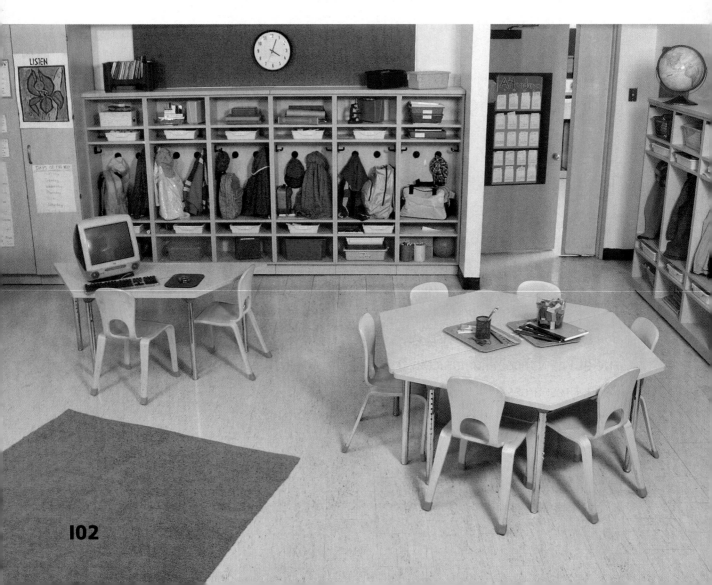

Everything you see is in its own location. A location can be large or small. Your chair is in a location. Your school is in a location. You are in a location!

This is a map of the same classroom. Maps make it easy to see the location of things.

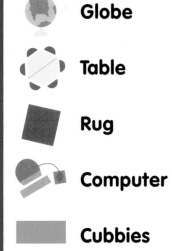

Map Key

Globe

Table

Rug

Computer

Cubbies

Grid Fun

A grid map can really help you find your way around!

A letter-number grid is a kind of map. All you need to find something on this map is one letter and one number. The letter tells you which column to look in. A column is a stack that you read from top to bottom. The number tells you which row to look in. A row is a line that you read from side to side.

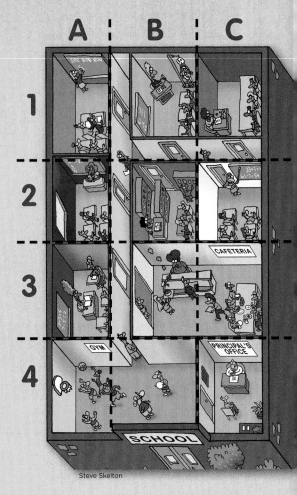

Steve Skelton

The kids at this colorful school never get lost. They use a grid map to find their way. Study the grid. Use your finger to find the places. Then answer the questions about each place.

1. Mr. Green's room is located at B-1 on the grid. What is hanging against the wall?

2. Ms. Blue's room is to the left of the cafeteria. What is the grid location for her class?

3. What is happening in grid locations A-4 and B-4?

4. Where is the red room on the grid?

Now look at this map of the western part of the United States. It uses a letter-number grid too. Find the places with your finger. Then answer the questions.

1. What are the grid locations for the state of California?
2. Which state is located at D5?
3. Which grid location do Montana and Wyoming share?
4. To travel in a straight line from North Dakota to the capital of Arizona, which grid locations would you go through?

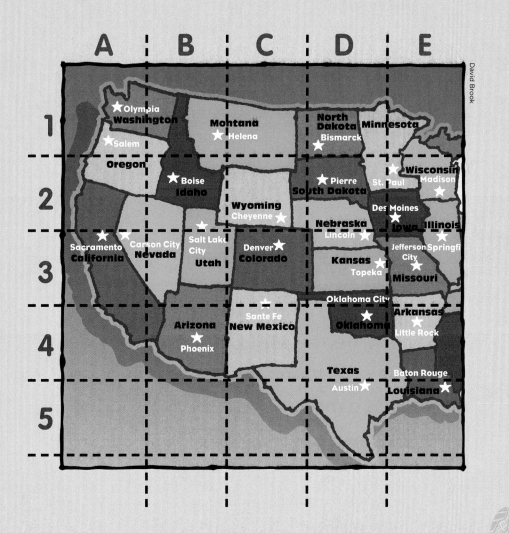

Description Writing Frame

Use the Writing Frame below to orally summarize "All About Location."

A map is a picture or drawing that shows things in certain places. The map of the classroom shows that

the globe _____

that are **by** _____ .

At the **bottom right** of the map you will find _____

_____ .

At the **bottom left** of the map you will find _____

_____ .

Each chair is **near** _____ .

Coats and books are **in** _____ .

The clock is **on** _____ .

Use the frame to write the summary on another sheet of paper. Be sure to include the **bold** signal words. Keep this as a model of this Text Structure.

Critical Thinking

1　The place or area where something can be found is called its _____.

    A. location

    B. look

    C. map

2　Describe a letter-number grid to a partner. Find sentences in "Grid Fun" that support your description.

3　Reread the information in "Grid Fun" that tell about columns and rows. Talk about this with a partner.

A map is a drawing that shows where different places are.

4　What does the map on page 103 show you? How is it the same and different from the map on page 104?

Digital Learning

For a list of links and activities that relate to this History/Social Science standard, visit the California Treasures Web site at www.macmillanmh.com to access the Content Reader resources.
Have children view the video "Exploring Our Earth."

North America

A large piece, or mass, of land is called a **continent**. Many countries make up the continent of North America. Canada is the largest country. El Salvador is the smallest country.

North America has many different kinds of landforms. There are huge mountains. The Rocky Mountains run all the way from Mexico to Alaska!

Three large oceans, the Atlantic, the Pacific, and the Arctic, surround our continent. Five Great Lakes, named Michigan, Huron, Erie, Ontario, and Superior, are located between Canada and the United States. There are also many rivers. One of the longest rivers in North America is called the Mississippi.

Title

Compass Rose

Map Scale

Map Key

Date

North America

ARCTIC
OCEAN

GREENLAND

ALASKA
(U.S.)

R O C K Y

N
W E
S

CANADA

Lake
Superior

Lake
Huron

Lake
Ontario

PACIFIC
OCEAN

M O U N T A I N S

SIERRA NEVADA
MOUNTAINS

Lake
Michigan

Missouri River

Mississippi River

Lake
Erie

APPALACHIAN MOUNTAINS

Colorado River

UNITED STATES

Ohio River

ATLANTIC
OCEAN

HAWAII
(U.S.)

SIERRA MADRE

MEXICO

CUBA

Map Scale

0   250   500 miles

BELIZE

HONDURAS

Map Key

GUATEMALA

NICARAGUA

Great Lakes

EL SALVADOR

Rivers

COSTA RICA

Mountains

PANAMA

Map made in 2007

Two Maps: One New, One Old

Maps help people describe the world.

Look at the two maps on these pages. One is more than 200 years old. The other is from today. They both show North America.

North America is a continent, or a large body of land. The United States is part of North America. So are Canada and Mexico.

Modern Map

Take a look at this map. It is a modern map of North America. Find the edges of the United States. The edge of a country is called a boundary. What are the names of the two countries that touch the United States? One is Canada. One is Mexico.

What bodies of water are at the edges of the United States? (Bodies of water can be oceans, gulfs, lakes, or rivers.)

On the East Coast is the Atlantic Ocean. To the south is the Gulf of Mexico. To the west is the Pacific Ocean.

Central Intelligence Agency/Library of Congress

Old Map

Take a look at this map. It was made in 1804. That's more than 200 years ago.

Use your finger to trace the boundaries of the United States on this map. Which of these 1804 boundaries is a boundary of the United States today? The Atlantic Ocean is still a boundary today.

There are some important differences between the modern map and the old map. One important difference is the size of the United States. It is much larger now. The boundaries of the United States have changed. It now stretches from the Atlantic Ocean to the Pacific Ocean. —*Susan Moger*

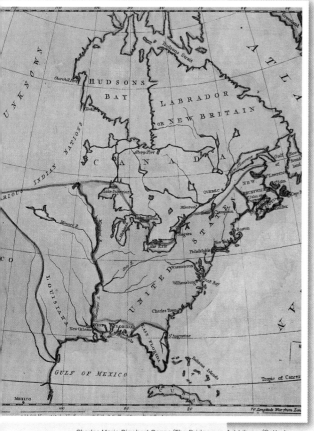

Charles Marie Rigobert Bonne/The Bridgeman Art Library/Getty Images

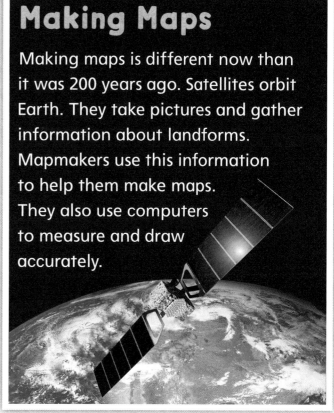

Making Maps

Making maps is different now than it was 200 years ago. Satellites orbit Earth. They take pictures and gather information about landforms. Mapmakers use this information to help them make maps. They also use computers to measure and draw accurately.

Deilev Van Ravenswaay/Photo Researchers

Compare/Contrast Writing Frame

Use the Writing Frame below to orally summarize "North America."

The countries on the map shown are **alike** in

many ways. They are **similar** because _____

_____ .

Canada, Mexico, and the United States **all share** _____

_____ .

The countries in North America are also **the same**

because they **all share** _____

_____ .

The countries of North America are **different** in
some ways.

Each country is a **different** _____

_____ .

Use the frame to write the summary on another
sheet of paper. Be sure to include the **bold** signal
words. Keep this as a model of this Text Structure.

Critical Thinking

1 A large piece or mass of land is called a

     _____ .

    A. continent

    B. Canada

    C. river

2 Find the sentences in "Two Maps: One New, One Old" that name the countries that touch the United States.

3 Find the information in this article about the new map. Then find the information about the old map.

4 With a partner, take turns describing what you see on the map of North America on page 109.

> A map is a drawing that shows where different places are.

Digital Learning

For a list of links and activities that relate to this History/ Social Science standard, visit the California Treasures Web site at www.macmillanmh.com to access the Content Reader resources.

Have children view the video "Exploring Our Earth."

Our Ancestors in California

Our ancestors came to California from all over the world.

The first people in California were the Native Americans. They lived on the coast and in the mountains, valley and desert. Jo's ancestors were Yurok Native Americans. Long ago, they lived on the coast of California. They were great fishers. Today Jo and his family still live on the California coast and follow many of the same **traditions** of their ancestors. A tradition is a special way of doing something that is passed down over time.

▼ A Yurok family today

Long after Native Americans came to California, many other people came. They came to find better lives for their families. They came to build homes and find good jobs and better schools.

When gold was found in California, thousands of people came hoping to become rich.

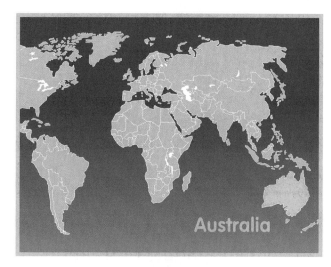

▲ Tim's ancestors traveled from Australia in 1851. They came to California to find gold.

▲ These immigrants came from Japan.

▲ Mae's ancestors traveled from Japan on a boat in 1890. They were farmers who came to California to grow fruits and vegetables.

COMING TO AMERICA

People come to the United States from all over the world for all kinds of reasons.

Millions of people live in the United States. Some of them came from other countries. They came for jobs. They came for adventure. They came for freedom.

Building America

Three hundred million people live in the U.S. Thirty-one million of them came here from other countries. They came to find a better life. They came in every year of our nation's history. In the 1840s a lot of people came from England, Germany, and Ireland. They worked on waterways. They worked on railroads. From 1890 to 1924 a lot of people came from Italy and Russia. They worked in factories. They helped build cities.

▼An Italian family in New York makes clothes, 1905.

AP Photo/Nick Ut

New Rules

Since 2001, there are new rules about who can come into the country. The rules help to protect the United States and keep out people who could do harm. It takes longer to come here, but people are coming. A new life is worth the wait.

Helping Out

People who come to the United States from other countries need a place to live. They need jobs. If the person's family is here, the family can help. The government helps, too, with health care and school. —*Joe MacGowan*

Where in the World Do They Come From?

Top 5 Places Where U.S. Immigrants Were Born (for the Year 2000)

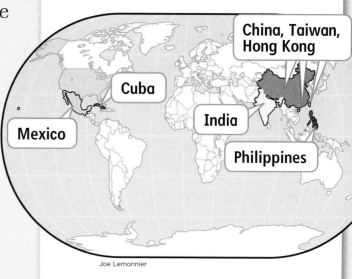

China, Taiwan, Hong Kong

Cuba

Mexico

India

Philippines

Joe Lemonnier

Cause/Effect Writing Frame

Use the Writing Frame below to orally summarize "Our Ancestors in California"

The first people to arrive in California were Native Americans. Some lived on the coast.

This lead to _____.

As a result, their ancestors _____

_____.

Because other people wanted to find better lives

for their families, _____.

The **effect** of this was that these people _____

_____.

When gold was found in California, the **effect** was _____

_____.

Use the frame to write the summary on another sheet of paper. Be sure to include the **bold** signal words. Keep this as a model of this Text Structure.

Critical Thinking

1 A way of doing something that is passed down over time is called a _____ .

    A. good job

    B. ancestor

    C. tradition

2 Find the sentences in "Coming to America" that tell how many people came here from other countries.

3 Point out the text in "Coming to America" that names the top 5 places where U.S. immigrants were born.

4 Compare the photographs of the immigrants on pages 116–117. How are they the same and different?

> A photograph is a picture taken with a camera.

Digital Learning

For a list of links and activities that relate to this History/ Social Science standard, visit the California Treasures Web site at www.macmillanmh.com to access the Content Reader resources.

Have children view the biography on John Muir, an immigrant from Scotland.

From City to Country

An **urban** community is a city, like San Francisco, California. The land is full of buildings, apartments, houses, and streets. You might find tall buildings. Many people work in these buildings.

▼ San Francisco is an urban area.

A **suburban** community is an area near a city. The *sub* in *suburb* means "near" and the *urb* means "city." A suburban community has open areas, like parks. Many people who work in a city live in nearby suburban areas.

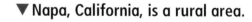
▲ Burlingame, California, is a suburban area.

A **rural** community is far from a city. *Rural* means "open land." There is a lot of land but only a few houses in a rural community. It is made up of small towns and farms and lots of land. Many California farms grow fruits and vegetables.

▼ Napa, California, is a rural area.

Whose Habitat Is It?

It can be a problem when people and animals have to share the same space.

In California, a cabin owner wrote to the Department of Fish and Game: "A bear . . . opened a refrigerator door, removed food, broke bottles, and carried a pound of bacon upstairs to a bedroom. In the process it left mud footprints and slobber all over the refrigerator."

AP Photo/Anchorage Daily News, Jim Lavrakas

▲ Black bears are not picky eaters!

   In almost every state, encounters between homeowners and wild animals are becoming more frequent. What's going on?

▼ Cities are spreading out into places where wild animals live.

Robert Fried/Alamy

FOR KIDS

Wild Life

When cities spread, open space disappears. This is called sprawl. Sprawl bothers plants and animals. About 2 million acres of open space are lost each year in the United States. When people move in, animals lose out.

Road Safety for All

Animals being hit by cars is another big problem. States and conservation organizations are working on this. Special overpasses and underpasses are being designed just to give animals a way across busy roads. Warning signs alert drivers to be on the lookout in areas where animals often cross roads. —*Kathryn Satterfield*

Something to Think About

Why is it important to give wild animals their space? How can we build homes for people and still protect animal habitats?

▼ An overpass just for animal traffic.

Robert McGouey/Alamy

Image Source/Getty Images

Compare/Contrast Writing Frame

Use the Writing Frame below to orally summarize "From City to Country."

The basic land use in California is **different** in three ways. Some areas are urban communities and full of

_____ .

In contrast, other areas are much less crowded.

Unlike the cities, rural areas _____ .

Unlike suburban areas, rural areas _____ .

Suburban communities are more **similar** to urban areas. People in a suburban community

_____ .

But a suburban community is **like** a rural community

in that _____ .

Use the frame to write the summary on another sheet of paper. Be sure to include the **bold** signal words. Keep this as a model of this Text Structure.

Critical Thinking

1 A community where there is a lot of land that is open is called _____.

   A. urban

   B. rural

   C. suburban

2 Find the part of the article in "Whose Habitat Is It?" that describes what can happen with black bears.

3 Read aloud the sentence in "Whose Habitat Is It?" that tells one way that animals lose their habitat.

4 With a partner, compare the photographs of the urban, suburban, and rural areas on pages 120-121.

A photograph is a picture taken with a camera.

Digital Learning

For a list of links and activities that relate to this History/ Social Science standard, visit the California Treasures Web site at www.macmillanmh.com to access the Content Reader resources.

Have children view the biography "Father of the Natural Park System."

Rules and Laws

Rules are made to keep people safe, help them get along with each other, and keep things fair. A rule for a community is called a **law**. Many countries have laws. Different countries often have different laws.

In the United States, the lawmakers are called **Congress**. These lawmakers make laws by writing bills. A bill is an idea for a new law. If Congress votes "yes" on a bill, it is given to the President. If the President agrees with the bill, it becomes a law. If the President does not like the bill, it goes back to Congress. If at least two thirds of the lawmakers there vote yes again, the bill becomes a new law.

▲ Congress in session

A trial is a meeting to decide if someone broke a law. In the United States, judges watch over **trials** in a court. Sometimes citizens, called a jury, are chosen to listen to a trial. A jury works with a judge to decide if someone broke a law and what is a fair punishment.

Not all countries have judges, juries, and trials. Some countries may have judges and trials, but no juries. Other countries have their own ways of carrying out laws, deciding if laws have been broken, and punishing those who go against the laws.

Too Young to Work

Kids are doing dangerous jobs on farms in the U.S. and around the world.

Valdemar Balderas was 12 when he started working. His home was in Texas, but every April his family went north to find farm work. They weeded sugar beets. They cleared rocks from fields. The workday began before the Sun rose and ended as it set. The family rarely got a day off.

▲ Valdemar Balderas and his parents

Forced to Work

All over the world, kids are forced to work. The total is about 250 million kids! They work in hard, often dangerous jobs. They work in mines. They weave rugs. They work in factories. More than 100 million of them work on farms. Many countries don't have laws to protect these kids.

▼ This 13-year-old boy works in a metal shop in Afghanistan.

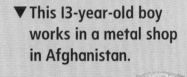

In the United States, a law requires safe working conditions for kids. It says how many hours kids can work. But the law does not apply to farm work.

A Dangerous Job

Farm work is dangerous for kids. They use sharp tools designed for adults. They run machines. They work near poisonous chemicals. More than 100,000 children are injured on farms each year.

Santos Polendo spent ten years working in the fields. He often had pain and headaches. "If you get hurt, there is no one to help," he says.

A Better Future

These farm workers are called migrants. That means they move often to find work. Kids leave school. When they go back, it's hard to catch up.

Santos stopped working in the fields. He finished high school. He is going to college to become an art teacher. One day he would like to have a family. He hopes his kids never have to work in the fields. —*Dina El Nabli*

Romano/Stolen Childhoods

▲ Working in an onion field in Texas

AP Photo/Pat Christman

▲ Children of farm workers need good school programs like this one.

129

Cause/Effect Writing Frame

Use the Writing Frame below to orally summarize "Rules and Laws."

In the United States, **when** Congress wants a new

law, _____ .

If Congress votes yes on a bill, the **effect** is that

_____ .

If the President agrees with the bill and signs it, **then** it

_____ .

If the President does not like the bill, **then** it

_____ .

When this happens, **if** at least two thirds of the
lawmakers there vote yes again, **then**

_____ .

Use the frame to write the summary on another
sheet of paper. Be sure to include the **bold** signal
words. Keep this as a model of this Text Structure.

Critical Thinking

1 A meeting to decide if someone broke a law is called a _____.

    A. bill

    B. rule

    C. trial

2 Read aloud the sentence in "Too Young to Work" that gives a reason why kids in many countries are forced to work.

3 Find the text in "Too Young to Work" that tells about a law for kids in the United States.

A caption is a title or an explanation of a photograph.

4 Which photograph in "Rules and Laws" shows Congress? Read aloud the caption.

Digital Learning

For a list of links and activities that relate to this History/ Social Science standard, visit the California Treasures Web site at www.macmillanmh.com to access the Content Reader resources.

Have children view the video "How Governments Work."

PEOPLE AND PLACES

Governments of Other Countries

Like the United States, Canada has a capital city. Canada's leaders, lawmakers, and judges meet in this city, Ottawa.

Canada

A long time ago, Canada was led by kings and queens. But today people **vote** for their leaders, as we do. When people vote, they make a choice, or say that they are for or against something.

The leader of Canada is called the prime minister. The lawmakers in Canada are called Parliament. Parliament is like Congress in the United States.

▲ Prime Minister
Stephen Harper
of Canada

▲ Canada's Parliament

132

Mexico is our neighbor to the south. Mexico and the United States share a border.

Mexico City is the capital of Mexico. Mexico's leaders, lawmakers, and judges meet in Mexico City. The lawmakers are called the Congress of the Union. They are like Congress in the United States.

▶ **Mexico**

As in the United States, the leader of Mexico is called the president. Mexico, however, votes for a new president every six years instead of every four years as the United States does.

▼ **President Felipe Calderon of Mexico**

▼ Mexico's Congress of the Union

Remembering Rosa Parks

Rosa Parks took a stand by taking a seat, and that made a big difference.

Bettmann/Corbis Images

▲ Rosa Parks sits in the front of the bus in 1956.

On December 1, 1955, Rosa Parks broke the law. It happened in Montgomery, Alabama. Her crime was to take an empty seat on a public bus. She refused to move when a white man wanted her seat. That doesn't seem like a crime today. But in 1955, laws in some states separated blacks and whites. This is known as segregation. In Montgomery, Alabama, separate seating was the law on buses.

FOR COLORED ONLY

Bettmann/Corbis Images

▲ Blacks and whites even had separate drinking fountains.

"We Won't Ride!"

Parks was arrested for not giving up her seat. That arrest set off a chain of events that changed the United States.

AP Photo/Gene Herrick

▲ Martin Luther King, Jr. is arrested in Montgomery.

African Americans in Montgomery took action. They refused to ride the buses. Martin Luther King, Jr., led the peaceful protest. The protesters stayed off Montgomery's buses for 381 days—more than a year.

The Law of the Land

In 1956 the U.S. Supreme Court ruled on the case. African Americans could not be forced to sit in certain areas on buses. In 1964 the Civil Rights Act was passed. It outlawed racial separation in all public places.

Mother of the Civil Rights Movement

Many people call Rosa Parks the mother of the civil rights movement. She led by example. She showed that peaceful protests work.

But Parks shared the credit for the important changes that took place. "The only thing that made it significant was that the masses of the people joined in," she said.

Rosa Parks quietly opened a new chapter in our nation's history. She died at age 92 in 2005. The world mourned her loss. —*Andrea Delbanco*

▼ Rosa Parks in 1999

Reuters/Corbis Images

Compare/Contrast Writing Frame

Use the Writing Frame below to orally summarize "Governments of Other Countries."

Like the United States, Canada has a _____.

Like people in the United States, people in Canada

_____.

In contrast to the United States, the leader of

Canada is _____.

Also **in contrast** to the United States, the lawmakers

in Canada _____.

Parliament is **like** _____.

Like the United States, Mexico has a _____.

The lawmakers in Mexico are **like** _____.

And **like** the United States, the leader of Mexico is

_____.

Use the frame to write the summary on another sheet of paper. Be sure to include the **bold** signal words. Keep this as a model of this Text Structure.

Critical Thinking

1 The act of making a choice, or when people say that they are for or against something, is called a _____.

   A. vote

   B. union

   C. congress

2 Find the text in "Remembering Rosa Parks" that tells how she broke a law.

3 Point out the sentences in this article that tell what happened to Rosa Parks after she broke a law.

4 With a partner, compare and contrast the maps on pages 132 and 133.

A map is a drawing that shows where different places are.

Digital Learning

For a list of links and activities that relate to this History/Social Science standard, visit the California Treasures Web site at www.macmillanmh.com to access the Content Reader resources.

Have children view the video "How Governments Work."

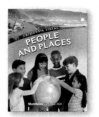

Countries Work Together

People in different countries sometimes work together to solve problems. For example, in 1965 too many polar bears were being hunted and killed. Since polar bears only live in Canada, Denmark, Norway, Russia, and the United States, people from these five countries had a meeting. They made a list of what they could do to help the polar bears.

In 1973 the countries signed a law to protect polar bears. Today the countries still work together to keep the polar bears safe.

In 1988 the leaders of England and France met to solve a problem. They wanted to build a tunnel under the English Channel to connect the two countries. They would call this tunnel the Chunnel.

Workers in France began to dig from their side. Workers in England began to dig from their side. Three years later the workers met in the middle. They had connected the two countries with the longest tunnel in the world.

The Chunnel was a huge **success**. When something is a success, it has a good ending or outcome. The English and French had wanted to make a tunnel for hundreds of years. By working together, they got the job done.

A machine used to dig the Chunnel

One Tough Job

Condoleezza Rice knew she wanted to make a difference in the world . . . and she did.

Jim Goldberg/Magnum Photos

▲ Rice is a big football fan.

Condoleezza Rice is the first African American woman to serve as U.S. Secretary of State. The secretary of state deals with leaders of other countries. It can be a tough job.

Working Hard

Condie Rice was born in 1954, in Birmingham, Alabama. She played classical music on the piano at 5. As a teen she was a talented ice-skater. She finished college at age 19.

Racism kept most African Americans out of top jobs when Rice was growing up. But her parents taught her that she could do anything. She planned to study music after college. Then she decided to make a difference in the world. She studied hard so she could do just that.

Before becoming secretary of state, Rice had other important jobs. She served on the National Security Council. She was the National Security Advisor to President George W. Bush from 2001 to 2005.

Mark Wilson/Getty Images

◄ Rice plays piano with famous cellist Yo-Yo Ma.

140

Travel and Tough Talk

The secretary of state meets with world leaders. Success is when the U.S. achieves its goals without war. In one year Rice took 18 trips to 33 countries. She traveled 247,603 miles. She handled problems with Afghanistan, Iran, Iraq, and North Korea. Rice believes that issues can be settled peacefully. Someone who knows her well once said, "She won't take no for an answer."

Olivier Doulliery/Abaca USA/Newscom

▲ Rice speaking at a news conference on the war in Iraq

Listening in the Middle East

The land dispute between Israelis and Palestinians has gone on for a long time. Finding a peaceful solution has been difficult. Sometimes it helps to listen. A secretary of state needs to be a good listener. Rice spent time in the Middle East listening to people. She said, "It was a good opportunity to come and to listen to people . . . [talk about] how they saw the future."

—Andrea Delbanco, Romesh Ratnesar, Elaine Shannon

AP Photo/Murad Sezer

▲ With Palestinian President Mahmoud Abbas

With the leaders of the Palestinian Authority and Israel ▶

David Silverman/Getty Images

Problem/Solution Writing Frame

Use the Writing Frame below to orally summarize "Countries Work Together."

In 1965, when there was the **problem** with polar

bears being killed, _____

_____.

To **solve** this polar bear **problem**, _____

_____.

As a result, today these countries _____.

In 1988, the leaders of England and France met to **solve**

a **problem**. They wanted to _____.

_____.

The **problem** was finally **solved** when _____

_____.

Use the frame to write the summary on another
sheet of paper. Be sure to include the **bold** signal
words. Keep this as a model of this Text Structure.

Critical Thinking

1 When something has a good or favorable ending or outcome, it is called a _____.

  A. problem

  B. state

  C. success

2 Find the sentence in "One Tough Job" that tells what the secretary of state does.

3 Read aloud the text on page 141 that tells what a secretary of state needs to be.

4 Describe the photograph of the machine on page 139. Talk about how it solved a problem.

A photograph is a picture taken with a camera.

Digital Learning

For a list of links and activities that relate to this History/ Social Science standard, visit the California Treasures Web site at www.macmillanmh.com to access the Content Reader resources.
Have children view the video "How Governments Work."

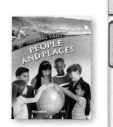

Farming Yesterday and Today

People from long ago worked hard to meet their needs. They hunted, fished, and picked plants every day. A group of people in a place called Mesopotamia made the first bread.

These people found grain that was good to eat. Grain is a seed found in plants such as wheat and rye. These people used stones to crush the grain to make flour. They added water to this. They cooked it over a fire to make bread.

Farmers planted some of the grain to grow more food. When there was no rain, the farmers brought water from nearby rivers to the plants.

▼ This art shows Mesopotamians tending crops.

144

Many years after the Mesopotamians, mills were invented. Mills are machines that crush things. At first, people had to work hard to turn a wheel on the mill to crush the grain into flour. Later, people figured out how to use water to turn the mill wheel.

▲ A mill with a water wheel

Today, **technology** is used to make things go faster, easier, better. Machines plant seeds and water them. Machines cut the plants that grow from the seeds. Machines pick out the grain and crush it. Machines do the work that people used to do by hand. Machines even help put flour in bags and send them to bakeries, grocery stores, and restaurants.

A machine for cutting plants ▼

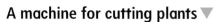
▲ A machine for planting seeds

Spinach Sleuths

Food detectives wanted to know why spinach was making people sick.

Raw spinach was in the news. E. coli (EE KO-lie) bacteria in the spinach had made people sick in 26 states. Three people died. The U.S. Food and Drug Administration (FDA) stepped in to stop the spread of disease.

Solving Puzzles

"Our job is detective work. A lot of science is solving . . . puzzles," Jack Guzewich says. He is a scientist with the FDA. "We try to figure out what . . . [is] making people sick. Then, we try to alert people so more people don't get sick. Finally, we try to . . . [make sure] it won't happen again."

During the spinach scare, scientists talked to people who got sick. All of them had eaten bagged spinach. That helped scientists track down the source of bacteria.

▲ FDA scientists collect samples from a field of spinach.

Inga Spence/Alamy

▲ Spinach growing in a California field

E. coli usually comes from the waste of people or animals. A team from the FDA looked into the ways the bacteria could have gotten into the spinach. They looked at how the spinach was watered. They looked at floods, fertilizer, nearby farm animals, and more.

At first, California spinach growers destroyed their crops. They knew that people would not buy fresh spinach for a while. Then the FDA announced that most fresh spinach was OK.

David Young-Wolff/Photo Edit

The Spinach Scare Is Over

After a while, people felt safe buying spinach again. Scientists think water from flooding may have caused the problem. Farmers and scientists are doing what they can to keep spinach safe from now on. —*Andrea Delbanco*

147

Sequence Writing Frame

Use the Writing Frame below to orally summarize "Farming Yesterday and Today."

People from **long ago** worked hard to _____.

The **first** people to make bread _____.

First these people _____.

Then these people _____.

After that, _____.

Finally they _____.

Many years **after** the Mesopotamians, _____

_____.

At **first** people _____.

Today _____.

Use the frame to write the summary on another sheet of paper. Be sure to include the **bold** signal words. Keep this as a model of this Text Structure.

Critical Thinking

1 The use of tools and machines to help produce something is called _____.

   A. teaching

   B. farming

   C. technology

2 Read aloud the text from "Spinach Sleuths" that tells what California spinach growers did to solve the spinach problem.

3 Point out the sentence from "Spinach Sleuths" that tells what scientists think caused this problem.

4 Discuss with a partner the captions on page 145 that tell about machines used today.

A caption is a title or an explanation of a photograph.

Digital Learning

For a list of links and activities that relate to this History/ Social Science standard, visit the California Treasures Web site at www.macmillanmh.com to access the Content Reader resources.

Have children view the video "Our Needs and Wants."

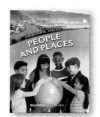

From Farm to Home

Long ago, people grew trees from seeds to get apples, but this took a long time. Today apples are grown on farms called **orchards**. And farmers today have a faster way to grow apples. They cut branches from a grown tree. They attach these branches to a young tree. This is called *grafting*. Soon flowers appear on the branches and turn into apples.

▼ Flowers grow on the branches.

▲ The farmer attaches branches to the new apple trees.

◄ The flowers turn into apples.

Just like long ago, when apples are ready to be picked today, people pick them by hand. And, like long ago, apple pickers today put the apples into sacks. The sacks are emptied into boxes. But unlike long ago, trucks are now used to bring the apples to a big refrigerator. This keeps the apples cold and fresh. Then the apples are washed and put into crates. Another truck carries the crates to a store.

▲ Apple pickers put the apples into sacks.

Boxes of apples are driven to a big refrigerator. ▶

Picking the Perfect Apple

Sometimes it's not easy to decide which apple to buy.

John Cloud was at a grocery store in New York City. He couldn't decide which apple to pick. One apple was organic. Organic food is grown without chemicals. That apple was from California.

The other apple was grown using chemicals. It was local. Local means nearby, within a few hours' drive. The local apple did not travel far to get to market.

The organic apple came from far away. It was in a refrigerated container to keep it cold. Cloud wondered how the apple would taste after its long, cold trip.

The New York apple came from nearby. It might taste better. Cloud bought both apples. They both tasted good.

Growing Food with Chemicals

Some farmers use chemicals to protect the foods they grow. In humid places the air often feels damp. Damp air makes harmful bacteria grow. Chemicals prevent bacteria from growing. Insects can also harm plants. Farmers use chemicals to kills insects.

Tom Hertz/Alamy

Organic or Local?

Many Americans buy organic foods. They prefer food that is grown without chemicals. Many shoppers buy local foods. They don't want to eat food from far away. It can be hard to find local food that is also organic. Shoppers have to choose. Scientists are still trying to decide which foods are healthier. One team studied tomatoes. They found that the organic tomatoes had more vitamin C. The same scientists studied two kinds of bell peppers. They did not find any difference.

(t to b) Photodisc/
Getty RF Collection;
foodfolio/Alamy

In Search of Local Food

John Cloud decided to buy food from a local farm. He joined a community-supported agriculture program. People pay a fee to join. Members get food from a local farm every week. The food is delivered to a central place. The members go and pick it up. Cloud gets fruit, eggs, and vegetables. —*Susan Moger*

AP Photo/Rita Beamish

Sequence Writing Frame

Use the Writing Frame below to orally summarize "From Farm to Home."

Long ago, people grew trees from _____.

Today farmers have a faster _____.

First a farmer _____.

Next a farmer _____.

Soon _____.

Long ago, when apples were ready to be picked, _____

_____.

Like **long ago,** apple pickers today _____

_____.

After that, trucks _____.

Use the frame to write the summary on another sheet of paper. Be sure to include the **bold** signal words. Keep this as a model of this Text Structure.

Critical Thinking

1 A farm where apples are grown is called an _____ .

   A. orchard

   B. orange

   C. old house

2 Find the sentence that tells what organic means in "Picking the Perfect Apple."

3 Use the text in "Picking the Perfect Apple" to talk with a partner about what John Cloud wanted to figure out.

4 Talk with a partner about the sequence of events in the diagram on page 150.

A diagram is a drawing or a plan. It explains the parts of something or the way it works.

Digital Learning

For a list of links and activities that relate to this History/Social Science standard, visit the California Treasures Web site at www.macmillanmh.com to access the Content Reader resources.

Have children view the video "Our Needs and Wants."

Producers and Consumers

A **producer** makes or grows a product, or good, to sell. A farmer is a producer. She grows a product such as grapes to sell.

The farmer might sell her grapes to a factory. There, workers make the grapes into jam to sell. These workers are also producers.

▼ This is a grape farm.

▼ This is a factory worker.

A **consumer** uses products or goods made by a producer. A consumer will buy grapes grown by the farmer and grape jam made by the factory workers.

Everyone is a consumer. That is because we all have needs and wants. When the farmer grows grapes to sell, she is a producer. But when she buys a piece of pottery that she wants, she is a consumer.

Kids in Charge

Some kids are bossy!

The kids in this story are bosses. They all have successful businesses. The National Foundation for Teaching Entrepreneurs helped them get started. An entrepreneur is a person who organizes and manages a project or business.

Business: LAVTweb
Laima Tazmin, president
New York, New York

Laima Tamzin began making Web sites when she was 7. She learned how from her brother's books. She started her company when she was 12. She designs Web sites for people and businesses. In one year she earned $25,000.

Arlen Tazmin

Cindy Hammond

Business: Shay's Bones and Biscuits
Shay Hammond, founder, owner, operator
Olive Hill, Kentucky

Shay's customers drool over her product. Why? They're dogs! When Shay was 11, she started selling homemade dog treats. She makes about $200 a year. Three stores sell her treats. She also sells them online.

illenberg

Business: ProPedder Kustoms
Buddy Dillenberg, chief executive officer
Birmingham, Alabama

Buddy Dillenberg saved up money to buy a car. But instead he bought machinery. That was the start of his business. His business makes cool add-ons for scooters. He sold them to his friends and online. Soon he was earning $1,000 a month!

Business: Baywear Legend
Luis Villa, chief executive officer
East Palo Alto, California

Luis Villa lived in a place where gangs and violence hurt people. When he was 14, Luis started a business to fight violence. His business makes belts, bandanas, and T-shirts. He takes gang colors and puts them with colors that say unity, or togetherness.

courtesy Build

Do You Want to Be Your Own Boss?

Here are five tips for starting a business.

Start Small
List your hobbies, then come up with a business idea for each one.

Listen Up
Get advice from an adult you can trust.

Mind Your Money
Keep track of what you earn and spend.

Always Deliver
Be honest.
Keep your promises.

Description Writing Frame

Use the Writing Frame below to orally summarize "Producers and Consumers."

A producer _____

_____ .

For instance, _____

_____ .

A farmer grows a product **such as** _____

_____ .

A grape farmer might, **for example,** _____

_____ .

A consumer _____

_____ .

Use the frame to write the summary on another sheet of paper. Be sure to include the **bold** signal words. Keep this as a model of this Text Structure.

Critical Thinking

1. Someone who makes or grows a product or good to sell is called a _____.

   A. pirate

   B. producer

   C. consumer

2. Point to the sentence in "Kids in Charge" that tells why Shay Hammond got started in her business.

3. Find the sentences in "Kids in Charge" that explain how Buddy Dillenberg earns $1,000 a month.

4. Discuss with a partner the photographs on pages 156 and 157.

> A photograph is a picture taken with a camera.

Digital Learning

For a list of links and activities that relate to this History/Social Science standard, visit the California Treasures Web site at www.macmillanmh.com to access the Content Reader resources.

Have children view the video "Our Needs and Wants."

Trading with Other Countries

In the United States we have a lot of factories and farmland. We make and grow many products. When we make and grow more goods than we need, we can trade the extra goods with other countries. We can give something we have a lot of to get something back that we need.

▲ Goods from another country

In the United States, we don't have the best **resources** to produce bananas. Resources are valuable materials or conditions belonging to a nation. Bananas grow only where it is hot and rainy, such as in the country of Panama. But consumers in the United States want bananas. So farmers grow bananas there and sell them to the United States.

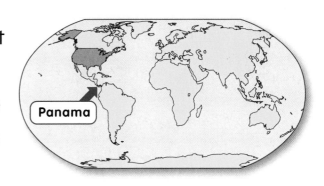

Panama

The United States produces a lot of sugar. Sugar producers sell sugar to consumers in the United States. They also sell sugar to Panama.

▼ Bananas are cut down in Panama and put on a boat.

▼ People in the United States enjoy eating bananas.

163

Kids Selling to Kids

For some young people, finding out what their friends like is a job.

Agent Jenny

Jenny Lieb is 16 years old. She lives in Florida. She hands out sticks of gum to her friends after lunch. She writes down what they think about the gum. Jenny is paid by a company called BzzAgent. They give her

▲ "Agent" Jenny Lieb, left, and her friend Susan Jacobs

Mark Wallheiser

products for free. Then she shares them with her friends. She gets paid for telling BzzAgent what her friends think about the product.

What Jenny does is called peer-to-peer marketing. This means that people try to get their friends to try products. BzzAgent has almost 100,000 agents like Jenny. Many of these agents are kids. The products include gum, soft drinks, music, movies, and more.

Yes, Billions

Why do companies like BzzAgent want to market to kids? Because kids spend money! Kids ages 12 to 19 spent $169 billion in one recent year.

Secret Agents?

Some kids keep their agent jobs secret. But Jenny has told her family and friends. Some leaders in the peer-to-peer business think agents should never be secret agents. —*Brenda Iasevoli*

▲ Kids are big spenders.

▲ Any secret agents here?

Should Kids Market Products to Their Friends?

Yes! Laura Groppe is the head of a peer-to-peer marketing company. The company talks to girls every week on its Web site. "Our

courtesy of Girls Intelligence Agency

agents can tell us if they hate a new product. The kids hold the power."

No! Juliet Schor is a professor at Boston College. She says, "When you tell a friend about a movie or product you like, that's great. But

courtesy Juliet Schor

when an adult asks you to promote a product, that's wrong."

Cause/Effect Writing Frame

Use the Writing Frame below to orally summarize "Trading with Other Countries."

In the United States, we have _____

_____ .

As a result, we _____

_____ .

When we make and grow more products than we

need, **then** _____ .

We can give something we have a lot of **in order**

to _____ .

Since the United States doesn't have the resources

to produce bananas, _____

_____ .

Use the frame to write the summary on another
sheet of paper. Be sure to include the **bold** signal
words. Keep this as a model of this Text Structure.

Critical Thinking

1 Valuable materials or conditions belonging to a nation are called _____.

    A. bananas

    B. rain

    C. resources

2 Find the sentence in "Kids Selling to Kids" that tells how much money kids ages 12 to 19 spent in one recent year.

3 Read aloud what Juliet Schor says about kids marketing products to their friends.

4 What does the map on page 163 show?

A map is a drawing that shows where different places are.

Digital Learning

For a list of links and activities that relate to this History/ Social Science standard, visit the California Treasures Web site at www.macmillanmh.com to access the Content Reader resources.

Have children view the video "Our Needs and Wants."

Nicholaus Otto

People Making Differences

Long ago it took days for people to get from one place to another. Then a man named Nicholaus Otto made an engine. An **engine** is a machine that turns energy into mechanical power or motion. Another man, Henry Ford, made a car that could run with Otto's engine.

Soon after, Mary Anderson found it hard to see out the car window when it rained. She made windshield wipers.

Henry Ford

These three individuals made a difference in the lives of people today.

Mary Anderson

Important discoveries have been made by scientists. Marie Curie was a scientist who discovered that something called radium can cure some illnesses. This treatment, called radiation, has saved many lives.

Albert Einstein was a scientist who was good at math. He helped inventors find ways of using large amounts of electricity all at once.

Albert Einstein

Marie Curie

Women Make History

Meet five women who have made their mark on history.

★★

Time Life Pictures/Getty Images

Sally Ride

In 1983, Sally Ride became the first U.S. woman in space. She served on the shuttle *Challenger*.

Quick Quote: "The thing that I'll remember most about . . . [my space] flight is that it was fun."

★★

Brendan McDermid/Reuters/Corbis

Effa Manley

Effa Manley was the first woman inducted into the Baseball Hall of Fame. She and her husband Abe owned an all-black baseball team. The team was the Newark Eagles. The time was the 1930s and 1940s. At that time black players and white players played on separate teams.

Quick Quote: "Abe . . . got the club together and I took care of the business details. It was a perfect partnership."

★ ★

Jack Reed/Reuters/Newscom

Nancy Pelosi

Nancy Pelosi is the first female Speaker of the U.S. House of Representatives.

Quick Quote: "It's a historic moment for the Congress; it's a historic moment for the women of America. It is a moment for which we have waited over 200 years."

★ ★

Marc Brasz/Corbis Images

Toni Morrison

In 1993, Toni Morrison became the first African American woman to win the Nobel Prize for literature.

Quick Quote: "If there is a book you really want to read, but it hasn't been written yet, then you must write it."

★ ★

AP Photo/Nasa

Eileen Collins

In 1999, Eileen Collins became the first woman to command a space shuttle mission.

Quick Quote: " My daughter just thinks that all moms fly the space shuttle. . . . In many ways I wish that a woman could have done this job at some point in the past. I feel like it's long overdue."

Sequence Writing Frame

Use the Writing Frame below to orally summarize "People Making Differences."

Long ago it took days for people _____

_____ .

Then _____

_____ .

Soon after that _____

_____ .

Then she _____ .

Important discoveries have also been made by _____

_____ .

Use the frame to write the summary on another sheet of paper. Be sure to include the **bold** signal words. Keep this as a model for writing a summary of this Text Structure.

Critical Thinking

1   A machine that turns energy into mechanical power or motion is called an _____.

   A. engine

   B. illness

   C. electricity

2   Point to Sally Ride's quote in "Women Make History." What did she think about her flight?

3   Read aloud the quote from Toni Morrison in the same article. What do you learn about her?

4   Look at the photographs of the people on pages 168 and 169. How did each person make a difference?

A photograph is a picture taken with a camera.

Digital Learning

For a list of links and activities that relate to this History/Social Science standard, visit the California Treasures Web site at www.macmillanmh.com to access the Content Reader resources.

Have children view the video "Many Special People."

Leaders for Freedom

Long ago when Abraham Lincoln was President, there was a war between the states in our country. The war was about slavery. **Slavery** is one person taking away another person's freedom.

President Lincoln was against slavery. He wrote an order that gave freedom to enslaved people in the South.

▼ Abraham Lincoln with soldiers

Sitting Bull was a Lakota Indian chief. Like Lincoln, Sitting Bull knew the importance of being free. Long ago many Native Americans were forced off their lands. The government wanted to make room for white people.

Sitting Bull knew this was not fair. He had the courage to fight for his people.

Susan B. Anthony believed that America would be a better place if all people were treated equally. She worked hard to change the law when women could not vote. She led marches and gave speeches.

▲ Sitting Bull

▲ Susan B. Anthony

Dr. King's Journey

Dr. Martin Luther King, Jr., dreamed that peace could change the world.

The Power of Protest

Every January we celebrate the life of Dr. Martin Luther King, Jr. He changed our nation. He believed all people should have the same rights.

Dr. King was born in Atlanta, Georgia, in 1929. At that time many laws kept black and white people apart. These laws were unfair. They made many people want change. During the 1950s, Dr. King and other leaders peacefully protested against those unfair laws. Dr. King believed in the power of protest without violence.

AP Photo

▲ In 1958, Dr. King leaves the hospital after recovering from a stab wound.

AP Photo

▶ Michigan, 1961: This bus station had separate waiting rooms for whites and blacks.

BUS DEPOT

WHITE WAITING —ROOM—

The March on Washington, 1963

In 1963, King led a march to Washington, D.C. A huge crowd of somewhere between 200,000 and 500,000 people of all races came. Dr. King's words that day still inspire people. He said, "I am happy to join with you today in what will go down in history as the greatest demonstration for freedom in the history of our nation."

Making History

After the march, Dr. King and other leaders met with President John F. Kennedy. This meeting helped get a law started. It was called the Civil Rights Act. The law said African Americans must have equal rights.

In 1964, Dr. King won the Nobel Peace Prize. The prize goes to people who try to bring peace and unity to the world.

▼ Dr. King (fourth from the left) meets with President Kennedy (fourth from the right) in 1963.

Hulton Archive/Getty Images

Compare/Contrast Writing Frame

Use the Writing Frame below to orally summarize "Leaders for Freedom."

Abraham Lincoln, Sitting Bull, and Susan B. Anthony were the **same** in that _____

_____ .

But Lincoln was **different** from Sitting Bull and Susan B. Anthony in that he was _____

_____ .

However, **like** Sitting Bull and Susan B. Anthony, Lincoln _____ .

Lincoln _____ .

Sitting Bull and Susan B. Anthony **both** _____

_____ .

Use the frame to write the summary on another sheet of paper. Be sure to include the **bold** signal words. Keep this as a model of this Text Structure.

Critical Thinking

1   One person taking away another person's freedom is called _____.

     A. war

     B. bravery

     C. slavery

2   Reread the sentence in "Dr. King's Journey" that tells when he was born.

3   What did Martin Luther King, Jr., win in 1964? Point to the sentence that states this.

4   Compare and contrast the pictures and the captions of Abraham Lincoln, Sitting Bull and Dr. Martin Luther King, Jr.

A caption is a title or an explanation of a photograph.

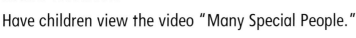

Digital Learning

For a list of links and activities that relate to this History/ Social Science standard, visit the California Treasures Web site at www.macmillanmh.com to access the Content Reader resources.

Have children view the video "Many Special People."

George Washington Carver

George Washington Carver was born on a farm in Missouri. George learned to love all growing things on the farm. People asked him to come to their houses to help their sick plants. They called George "The Plant Doctor."

When George tried to go to **college**, he was turned away because of the color of his skin. A college is a place that provides a higher level of education. George had great courage. He went on to find another college. There he studied hard and became a great scientist. He discovered over 300 ways to use peanuts, including how to make peanut butter.

Golda Meir

Golda Meir was a great leader. When she was 70 years old, she became the prime minister of Israel. Israel is a country in the continent of Asia.

Golda was Jewish. She was born in Russia. Many Jewish people in Russia were not treated fairly. When she was eight years old, her family moved to the United States.

When she was an adult, Golda decided to help Jewish people from all over the world. She had meetings with other Jewish people. They made a plan to go back to Israel, a land where Jewish people had lived long ago.

Golda Meir was the prime minister of Israel from 1969 to 1974. ▶

Their Stamp on History

Every year, the U.S. Postal Service issues stamps to honor important African Americans. Here are some of the people who have been honored.

Sojourner Truth

She was born into slavery in 1797. Later, after becoming free, she traveled around the Northeast and Midwest. She spoke out against slavery and in favor of women's rights.

In Her Own Words

"I have a right to have just as much as a man."

Harriet Tubman

She helped hundreds of slaves escape to freedom between 1850 and 1860. She helped them escape to the North where they would be free. The secret route she led them on was called the Underground Railroad. The people she helped were called "passengers."

In Her Own Words

"I never ran my train off the track, and I never lost a passenger."

W.E.B. DuBois

In 1909, this writer started an organization that still helps African Americans today.

In His Own Words

"The human soul cannot be permanently chained."

W.E.B.DuBois
29
Black Heritage USA

Bessie Coleman

In 1921, she became the first African American to get a pilot's license.

In Her Own Words

"I refused to take no for an answer."

BLACK HERITAGE
USA 32
BESSIE COLEMAN

Jackie Robinson

In 1947, he became the first African American to play modern Major League Baseball.

In His Own Words

"There's not an American in this country [who is] free until every one of us is free."

Jackie Robinson
Black Heritage USA 20c

Cause/Effect Writing Frame

Use the Writing Frame below to orally summarize "George Washington Carver" and "Golda Meir."

Because George Washington Carver was born on

a farm, he _____

_____ .

Since he was able to help people's sick plants, _____

_____ .

When George tried to go to college, _____

_____ .

But he had great courage. **As a result,** _____

_____ .

Golda Meir was a great leader. **As a result,** _____

_____ .

Use the frame to write the summary on another sheet of paper. Be sure to include the **bold** signal words. Keep this as a model of this Text Structure.

Critical Thinking

1 A place that provides a higher level of education is called a _____ .

    A. country

    B. college

    C. family

2 Find the sentences in "Their Stamp on History" that tell what Sojourner Truth did.

3 Point out where in "Their Stamp on History" you can find a quote from Jackie Robinson.

4 Point to the photographs of George Washington Carver and Golda Meir on pages 180 and 181.

A caption is a title or an explanation of a photograph.

Digital Learning

For a list of links and activities that relate to this History/ Social Science standard, visit the California Treasures Web site at www.macmillanmh.com to access the Content Reader resources.

Have children visit the biography "George Washington Carver."

Acknowledgments

Illustration Acknowledgments

19: Christine Schneider. 30: Sue Carlson. 55: Sam Tomasello. 60–61: Susan Trimpe. 102: Peggy Tagel

Photography Acknowledgments

All photos for Macmillan/McGraw-Hill except as noted below:

Cover: Karl Ammann/CORBIS. 6: Jane Burton/Dorling Kindersley/Getty Images. 7: Ken Lucas/Getty Images. 12: (cl) Photodisc/Getty Images; (c) Photodisc/Getty Images; (cl) Photodisc/Getty Images. 13: (tcr) Norbert Schaefer/CORBIS; (bl) Rolf Bruderer/CORBIS; (br) Spencer Grant/Photo Edit; (cr) Steve Cole/Photodisc Red/Getty Images. 18: Kevin R. Morris/CORBIS. 24: Photolibrary.com Pty. Ltd./Index Stock Imagery. 25: Tim Ridley/Dorling Kindersley. 31: (tr) © JBJ Productions/zefa/CORBIS; (cr) O'Brien Pictures/Jupiter Images; (bl) Photofusion Picture Library/Alamy. 36: (bcl) Brand X Pictures/PunchStock; (br) Gary Crabbe/Alamy; (bl) Papilio/Alamy; (bc) Siede Preis/Getty Images. 37: Brand X Pictures/PunchStock. 42: (bcl) Don Vail/Alamy; (bcr) David Boag/Oxford Scientific/Jupiterimages; (bcl) Hans Pfletschinger/Peter Arnold. 43: (bcr) Zigmund Leszczynski/Animals Animals-Earth Scenes; (tcl) John T. Fowler/Alamy; (tc) PHOTOTAKE Inc./Alamy; (tcr) DIOMEDIA/Alamy; (cl) Papilio/Alamy; (tr) John P. Marechal/Bruce Coleman. 48: (tcr) Tom Silver/CORBIS; (tr) Daniel J. Cox/CORBIS; (b) Mark Raycroft/Minden Pictures. 49: Tom & Pat Leeson/Ardea London Ltd. 54: (tr) Maryann Frazier/Photo Researchers, Inc.; (b) Theo Allofs/zefa/CORBIS. 55: Fabrice Bettex/Alamy. 66: (tr) Harry Taylor/Dorling Kindersley; (b) Colin Keates/Dorling Kindersley, Courtesy of the Natural History Museum, London. 67: (tcr) Colin Keates/Dorling Kindersley, Courtesy of the Natural History Museum, London; (c) wsr/Alamy. 72: David Keaton/CORBIS. 73: Boris Karpinski/Alamy. 78: (cr) Don Farrall/Getty Images; (bcl) geogphotos/Alamy. 79: (cr) Maurice Harmon/Graphistock/PictureQuest; (br) Matt Meadows/Peter Arnold, Inc.; (cl) Franck Jeannin/Alamy; (bcl) Mark & Audrey Gibson/Stock Connection (IPNStock). 84: (tr) Layne Kennedy/CORBIS; (b) Francois Gohier/Gaston Design/Photo Researchers, Inc. 85: Ken Lucas/Visuals Unlimited. 90: (c) PhotoLink/Getty Images; (bl) Michael S. Yamashita/CORBIS; (bc) Juliette Wade/Dorling Kindersley; (br) Lester V. Bergman/CORBIS. 91: (tr) davies and starr/Getty Images; (b) Bettmann/CORBIS. 96: Fred Ramage/Hulton Archive/Getty Images. 97: (bl) Corbis; (bcl) Corbis; (bcr) Getty Images/Blend Images RR; (br) Superstock; (cr) Photodisc/Alamy. 115: (cl) Bettmann/CORBIS; (br) MIXA/Getty Images; (tr) Image Source Pink/Getty Images. 120: Mark E. Gibson/MIRA: Media Image Resource Alliance. 121: (tr) Mark Gibson/Index Stock Imagery; (b) Robert Glusic/Photodisc/Getty Images. 126: Dennis Cook/AP. 127: Comstock Production Department/Comstock Images/Alamy Images. 132: (bl) Tom Hanson/CP/AP-Wide World Photos; (bcr) Chris Wattie/Reuters/CORBIS. 133: (b) Jorge Uzon/AFP/Getty Images; (cr) © Marcos Delgado/epa/CORBIS. 138: Creatas/Dynamic Graphics Group/Alamy Images. 139: (b) qaphotos.com/Alamy Images; (tr) © Reuters/CORBIS. 144: (cr) D. Hurst/Alamy Images; (b) © Archivo Iconografico, S.A./CORBIS. 145: (tr) © David Muench/CORBIS; (bl) © Tom Bean/CORBIS; (br) Peter Dean/Agripicture Images/Alamy Images. 150: (cl) Larry Lefever/Grant Heilman Photography, Inc.; (cr) James P. Blair/Photodisc Green/Getty Images; (bc) Royalty-Free/CORBIS. 151: (tr) Michael Melford/The Image Bank/Getty Images; (b) Walter Hodges/CORBIS. 152: Burke Triolo Productions/Getty Images. 156: (cl) J.A. Kraulis/Masterfile; (cr) Pictor International/Image State/Alamy Pictures/Alamy; (cl) Ryan McVay/Getty Images. 157: (br) Eddie Stangler/Index Stock Photography; (b) Rick Sullivan/Bruce Coleman, Inc. 162: Ian Murphy/Stone/Getty Images. 163: (br) Danny Lehman/CORBIS; (bl) Juan Silva/Getty Images. 168: (cr) Bettmann/CORBIS; (tr) Bettmann/CORBIS; (br) Kim Mould/Omni-Photo Communications, Inc.; (bl) Courtesy Birmingham Public Library Archives, Portrait Collection. 169: (l) Hulton Archive/Getty Images; (r) Courtesy of the Archives, California Institute of Technology. 174: Bettmann/CORBIS. 175: (tr) CORBIS; (br) CORBIS. 180: Stock Montage/Hulton Archive/Getty Images. 181: (tl) David Rubinger/Time Life Pictures/Getty Images; (br) Popperfoto/Alamy Images

186